Cli...

St Andrews
and the Islands

St Andrews
and the Islands

Ronald Rees

Photographs: Tom Moffatt

NIMBUS
PUBLISHING LTD

To the memory of David Rose.

Nimbus Publishing Limited
PO Box 9301, Station A
Halifax, NS B3K 5N5
(902) 455-4286

Design: Doug Porter, Virtual Image Productions, Halifax
Map reprinted with permission
Printed and bound in Canada

Canadian Cataloguing in Publication Data
Rees, Ronald, 1935-
St Andrews and the Islands
Includes bibliographical references
ISBN 1-55109-115-1
1. St. Andrews (N.B.)—History. 2. Passamaquoddy Bay Region (N.B. and Me.) — History. I. Moffatt, Tom. II. Title.

FC2499.S13R43 1995   971.5'33   C95-950011-1
F1044.5.S13R43 1995

Contents

Jane Crosen, mapmaker

FOREWORD ↜

TRAVELLERS WHO TURN OFF THE HIGHWAY from Calais (Maine) to Saint John (New Brunswick) and head down the peninsular road to St Andrews, quickly become aware of a change of landscape. Stretches of hayfield and pasture replace cut-over spruce woods and run in long swaths down to a broad river. The river road, as route 127 is known locally, parallels the shore of the St Croix on its last few miles to the ocean. Just above St Andrews the river empties into Passamaquoddy Bay, a great inlet of the Bay of Fundy and the Atlantic, whose waters lap the southern end of the peninsula. As you enter the town, the road bends sharply and tilts, propelling you toward the shore. Within moments you are in a marine environment, your feet still on land but your senses filling with the sight, sounds and smells of the sea. The continent has been left behind. Walk onto the town wharf or to the tip of the peninsula and you discover the extent of your envelopment. The town is girded by water.

Looked at on a map, St Andrews is at the centre of a wheel of water. A few miles to the west is the coast of Maine, to the east is New Brunswick's Mascarene shore, and to the south the islands that crowd the mouth of Passamaquoddy Bay: Deer Island, Moose Island or Eastport, and Campobello. Beyond these, guarding the entrance to the Bay of Fundy itself, is Grand Manan. Linked by name, legend, and, until recently, by commerce, the peninsula and islands are a neighbourhood, albeit one divided by an international boundary and a time zone. British officials sometimes described the whole as the Archipelago, Americans as Passamaquoddy or Quoddy, names which—the British would not have failed to register—they interchanged with that of Eastport itself. The collection district of Passamaquoddy, established by act of Congress in 1791, still retains the name. The islands are also linked by legend. One day the ancient Micmac spirit Glooscap saw a moose and a deer being chased by a pack of wolves in the waters of the Bay. As the moose and deer swam towards shore, the wolves began to close in so Glooscap, to save the doomed animals, changed them into islands. When all traffic was by water, the peninsula and the islands were connected formally by mail packets, ferries, and scheduled steamers, and informally by the flotilla of fishing vessels, sloops and schooners that plied the waters of the Bay. When Eastport—the last American town to be occupied by British troops—raises the roof on its celebrated Independence Days, its harbour is filled with boats from Deer Island and Campobello. Until well into this century, there were regular steamship runs from Boston to Eastport, with connections to St Andrews, St Stephen, Calais and Saint John. But the steamships have now gone and the ferries between the islands run only seasonally. None leave from St Andrews. The ferry to Grand Manan, St Andrews' last direct link with the islands, now leaves from Black's Harbour, a town twenty miles closer to Saint John but one with which Grand Manan had no historical links.

Yet in spite of the loss of ferries, mail packets and steamers, there is still a sense of connectedness. A bi-weekly newspaper, the *St. Croix Courier,* serves communities on both the American and Canadian sides of the St Croix river, and the engaging *Quoddy Tides,* published fortnightly in Eastport, Maine, is directed at communities in and around Passamaquoddy Bay: Eastport itself, its neighbour Lubec, Robbinston, St Andrews, Campobello, Deer Island and Grand Manan. Mailings take place at Eastport and St Stephen, New Brunswick. Tide times are given in Atlantic (Canadian) time, and sunrise/sunset times in Eastern (US) time.

There is, too, a Canadian/American tourism association, a Border Historical Society, with its Border History publications series, and (at Eastport) an International House. If you live in a valley on the eastern side of Eastport, and have no satellite or cable reception, your television programming is limited to Canadian broadcasting along with Maine public broadcasting. Viewers without cable on the Canadian side pick up Canadian channels and public broadcasting from Maine. All are small but persistent reminders of a reality that central governments are disposed to ignore: that the Quoddy region may straddle an international boundary but it is a social and geographic unity.

THE SETTLERS

*I*N THE ST CROIX River, about four miles above St Andrews, there is a small mid-stream island given official status by a flagpole that, on the New Brunswick shore, is just visible from the highway. Travellers unfamiliar with the history of the area and curious about the flagpole might guess that the island had once been a summer camp for aboriginal fishermen, or perhaps an emplacement for British troops guardingthe entrance to the river. Nothing quite so humdrum. If they persist with their inquiries, they will discover that the island was nothing less than the site of the first European attempt at year-round settlement on the Atlantic seaboard north of the Spanish settlements in Florida. The year was 1604. For public information on the island settlement, travellers on the New Brunswick side have to drive ten miles upriver to the bridge at Calais/St Stephen and then downstream to the park on the Maine shore where there is a look-out, a picnic ground, and a plaque with a full and informative legend. The Island is on the American side of the line.

The first European residents of St Croix Island were a company of French explorers and adventurers led by Count, or Sieur, de Monts and Samuel de Champlain. Armed with a commission from Henry IV of France, de Monts and Champlain—the expedition's navigator, cartographer, and chronicler—set sail from Havre de Grace in the spring of 1604 for La Cadie, the region of North America between the 40th and 46th parallels. Their aim was to colonize and govern, and to provide enough furs to satisfy the expedition's merchant backers in La Rochelle, Rouen and Toulon. After the crossing they spent about a month looking for a coastal base from which to launch the colony, and in late June they settled for an island about four miles above the mouth of a broad river whose waters, a little farther upstream, meet in the form of a cross. They named the river Saincte Croix, and the island after the river. The island, about 300 yards long by 125 wide, commanded the mouth of the river and, being small, could easily be defended against attacks from either bank.

Once ashore, Champlain, who had seen most of the Spanish towns in the Americas, drew up a plan for the settlement. Two drawings have survived, one a ground plan and the other a perspective view showing his designs for the buildings and gardens. All were neatly arranged around a central square; the gardens, rectangular and with straight paths, lying just beyond the buildings. Work began immediately, the men being assigned "to fetch wood, to cut timber, [and] to carry earth." Buildings were made with local timber and with planks, doors and windows brought from France in the ship's hold.

It is unlikely that the island settlement ever resembled Champlain's plans for it, but the expedition built storehouses and living quarters, planted gardens on the mainland as well as in the poor, sandy soil of the island, and established defences in case the Indians proved to be hostile. But the enemy that undid the Frenchmen was not Indians, outraged at the intrusion, but winter, harsher then than now, and malnutrition. The 17th century was a period of generally colder winters, the "Little Ice Age," when Alpine glaciers grew in length and the Thames and the Dutch canals froze regularly.

St Croix (also Dochet's) Island, site of the first European attempt at permanent settlement on the Atlantic seaboard north of the Spanish settlements in Florida. Before winter set in and pack ice choked the river, the French settlers drew water from the stream.

On the island at the mouth of the St Croix the winter of 1604-05 began early. Snow fell in October and by the end of the following April it was still three to four feet deep; there were few thaws. North winds swept down the river, freezing, in the absence of protective cellars, all the "liquors" except the Spanish wine; barreled cider, brewed in Normandy, had to be dispensed by the pound. By early December, the river was so filled with ice that it became difficult, and at times impossible, to fetch wood and water from the mainland. An island that in

June had seemed a haven had become a prison.

Though flanked by dense woods, the hapless colonists—who had used much of the island's wood to make buildings—ran short of fuel. Unable to store vegetables, they were quickly reduced to a diet of salted meat and, there being no fresh water on the island, melted snow. Scurvy ravaged the company. Gums rotted and fell away, teeth loosened, legs and arms became swollen and hard, and the breath shortened. By spring thirty-four of the company of seventy-nine who remained on the island had died and twenty more barely escaped death. The only men to escape unscathed—in a misadventure that became a cautionary tale—were the dozen who did not sit indoors: a "jolly company of hunters," according to an account written a few years later, "who preferred rabbit hunting … [and] making snowballs to bring down the game to sitting around the fire talking about Paris and its good cooks."

But not even a jolly company of snowballing hunters relished the prospect of another winter on the St Croix. Ignorant, too, of the origins of disease, they were also anxious to escape the poisonous humours or miasmata that they believed must emanate either from the river or from the soils of the island. The French name for scurvy is *mal de la terre.* When the relief ship arrived in the middle of June, 1605, both they and their chastened companions abandoned the settlement and crossed the Bay of Fundy to Port Royal, a sheltered site at the mouth of the Annapolis valley in Nova Scotia that they had noted in their reconnaissance of the previous summer.

With the departure of the French, control of the river and the Bay reverted to its aboriginal inhabitants, the Passamaquoddy Indians. The Passamaquoddies were members of the Wabanaki nation or confederacy whose name signified "people of the east," or "people who live nearest the dawn." Expert canoeists, the Passamaquoddies fished in the river and the bay, and dug or gathered clams on the flats. The clams were placed in an oven and cooked just enough to be easily taken out of their shells. They were then dried on sticks and, thus preserved and easy to carry, they were a source of winter food and salt.

Though primarily a hunting and fishing tribe, the Passamaquoddies also

planted corn and probably grew a little tobacco. In winter they moved to sheltered quarters inland and up-river where moose and deer were plentiful. According to a sympathetic French missionary, Father Biard,

Indian midden, Oven Head, near St Andrews. In summer, Passamaquoddy Indians fished and hunted sea mammals and birds; they also shucked and ate clams, the shells piling up near the encampment.

they loved justice, hated violence and robbery, and were liberal and generous. They neither threatened the French settlement nor pillaged it after the island had been abandoned. Yet in skirmishes with rival tribes they could be ferocious, on occasion carrying off the heads of their enemies.

Eventually their health and culture would be destroyed by that destructive European triad—rum, trade goods, and disease—and their hunting grounds decimated by woodsmen and farmers. But they were spared the ravages of European contact for a century or more by occupying territory on the margins of the two bases of European power. French interests lay in the St Lawrence valley and the fur-rich hinterland, British in the thirteen colonies along the eastern seaboard. For both the French and the English, the Passamaquoddy region, and

Acadia (La Cadie) as a whole, was a no-man's land. Strategically useful to both sides as a buffer against the aggression of the other but coveted by neither, it was passed back and forth between the two great powers. In 1621, during a period of British dominance, James I of England (and IV of Scotland) declared all the land between the Gaspé and the St Croix to be a fief of Scotland. The region itself he renamed Nova Scotia, and the St Croix, its southern boundary, the Tweed. The St Croix remained the St Croix but the name Nova Scotia eventually took hold even though in the early 17th century the region was of no interest to Scottish or English settlers.

But perceptions of utility are notoriously hostage to circumstance. After the fall of Quebec in 1759 a once-shunned borderland became a region of opportunity. With the French threat removed, dangerous Acadia became hospitable Nova Scotia. New Englanders looked with new eyes at the resources of the north. To trade with the Passamaquoddies and catch and dry the cod, haddock and pollock that swarmed in the plankton-rich cold waters, they set up summer camps on Indian Island and Deer Island at the mouth of the Bay. Passamaquoddy is an Indian word meaning the bay where the pollock are. Also, land was granted to English army and navy officers but most of the recipients made no effort to settle on their grants or persuade others to do so.

CAMPOBELLO AND THE OWENS ♒

OF THE PASSAMAQUODDY GRANTS all were forfeited save one: the William Owen grant in Campobello. Owen, a Welshman and a lieutenant in the British navy, had an arm shot off at the battle of Pondicherry, India, during the Seven Years' War, and at the end of the war he petitioned what he hoped would be a grateful Admiralty for a "gratuity, pension or preferment." Receiving only a "pitiful" pension that would have sentenced him to life, he poignantly recorded, "among my relations for the remainder of my days," he turned to his former commander in India, Sir William Campbell. Sir William, who had just been appointed

Captain William Owen's beautiful
meadow—Campobello.

governor of Nova Scotia, was more forthcoming than the naval lords, and in 1766 Owen found himself in Halifax, promoted to captain, and serving as a voluntary aide to the governor. A year later, as a reward for his services in India and Nova Scotia, Owen and his three nephews, Arthur, David and William Owen—the reward being too great for a single grantee—received from Sir William the grant of the Great Outer Island of Passamaquoddy. Owen's title, Principal Proprietary, was equally grandiloquent. To both honour his patron, Sir William Campbell, and acknowledge the natural beauty of the island, Owen renamed it Campobello. Yet Owen, possibly expecting more, was slow to take possession. He went back to Britain in the fall of 1767, toured France and the Netherlands, and lost an eye in an election brawl at Shrewsbury in England. For the rest of his life he wore a black patch tied with a ribbon to the queue of his hair. Only in the late summer of 1768 did he and a group of friends and associates address the problem of settling Campobello. At a coffee house in Warrington, Lancashire, they agreed to form a colonization company and authorized Owen to buy a ship and find settlers. In February 1769, Owen bought a snow, a brig-like vessel, and a month later left Liverpool for Campobello under the command of Captain Plato Denny, one of the shareholders of the colonization company. Aboard the snow (named *Snow Owen*) were thirty-eight colonists, most of them indentured servants, who in exchange for free passage committed themselves to several years of unpaid labour. So that his infant colony might survive without, as he noted in his diary, "the calling of any auxilliary," Owen chose his servants carefully. Among them were weavers, masons, brickmakers, potters, butchers, barbers, and ploughmen. At Owen's disposal, too, was the "cheerful assistance on all occasions" of the fifteen member crew of the *Snow Owen*. Later, Owen advertised in Liverpool and Boston for unindentured colonists, offering a free passage, a ninety-nine year lease, a house, outbuildings, a fifty-acre lot, and a loan for the purchase of six cows, two oxen, a sow pig, and access to all timber under twelve inches square.

As an 18th century naval captain in charge of reluctant and sometimes unruly émigrés, Owen's rule of the island was inevitably firm and—for the sluggards and backsliders—mercifully brief. He put up a "wiping post" and built stocks in which at least one offender—a man caught stealing rum—had both to sit and, Owen's diary reveals, wear a sign that labelled him a thief, a liar, and a drunkard. But an island run as a tight ship paid dividends. In just over a year his motley group, guided by several families of able New Englanders who had moved onto the island, had built houses, a grist mill, a church, made kitchen gardens, planted orchards, drained marshes, cleared and fenced land for hay, oats and potatoes, and shipped lumber and potash to Britain. Though the New Englanders had no legal right to be on the island they were welcomed by the astute Captain Owen. The women knew how to run households in a wilderness, and each of the men was that now-familiar Maritime mixture: a carpenter, farmer, fisherman and seaman.

Owen, who clearly hankered for the Old World, left for England in the fall of 1771, never to return. (He rejoined the navy and was killed in India in 1778). Most of the émigrés quickly followed his lead and within months of his departure, twenty-seven of the thirty-eight persuaded Owen's deputy on the island, Captain Plato Denny, to let them return to England on the *Snow Owen*. Many had left families and all were homesick. The crew of the snow might also have been anxious to go home. Late in 1772 the ship set sail for Liverpool but there would be no happy homecoming: the ship, its cheerful crew, and all passengers were lost at sea. On Campobello, the vacuum left by the departed émigrés was filled by New Englanders already on the island who had collected in a settlement known subsequently as Wilson's Beach, and others from the mainland. But Campobello had not seen the last of the Owens. In 1787, nine years after his uncle's death, one of the co-grantees, thirty-three year old David or "Squire" Owen, turned up to claim his inheritance. David Owen had been a fellow at Trinity College, Cambridge, and a tutor to William Pitt, the future prime minister of England.

    As David Owen's sobriquet suggests, he brought to the New World many of the worst features of the Old, among them an

The Owen House, Campobello, built c. 1835 by Admiral William FitzWilliam Owen, David Owen's successor as principal proprietary of the Island.

18th century sense of property. Owen's world was one of leases, tenancies and landlord's rights. He built a large house, Ty'n-y-Coed (House in the Woods), near the site of the present Roosevelt cottage, and demanded that settlers on the island pay him rent or leave. He spent much of the rest of his life trying to evict the New England "squatters" or "trespassers" who not only refused to move but, having made most of the improvements on the island, also insisted on gaining title to their land. The Wilson's Beach settlement he always referred to as "the Wilson Encroachment."

Apart from the New Englanders at Wilson's Beach, who eventually won their battle for title, everyone else was Owen's tenant, and though rents were not high—and in difficult times were often paid in dried fish and potatoes—the tenancies were restrictive. Many of the leases ran from only four to seven years and they were applied to lands adjacent to fishing weirs as well as farmlands and pastures. An acre of land at Clarke's Beach, leased in 1804, cost Jonathan Parker fifty shillings a year for the following ten years. Tenants who strayed beyond the boundaries of their leases forfeited their "penal bonds," and debtors and defaulters faced eviction. Among the latter was Jonathan Parker who, had he not been supported by the Wilson's Beach settlers, might have been turned out of his house in 1816.

When Captain Gustavus Nicolls, a military engineer on board His Majesty's Schooner *Hunter,* visited Campobello in 1808 he was clearly puzzled by the feudal-like conditions on an island at the threshold of an empty continent. He considered Campobello to be "much the finest" island in the Bay and that it would have been in "a flourishing state" had the land been sold to the settlers. But, he continued, "it cannot be supposed that people will flock to an Island where the ground is only let to them for a certain number of Years, which after being cleared & improved, is at the expiration of that time to revert to the Owners."

Even the Indians on Campobello suffered the ignominy of property. They were allowed to take birch or other bark only on condition that they did not injure the trees or carry away timber. When David Owen died, in 1829, his body—as he had requested—was placed in a lead coffin filled with spirits and shipped across the Atlantic for burial in Wales. A cruel rumour had it that the sailors drank the spirits and threw the body into the sea.

St Andrews and the Loyalists ᴥ

While David Owen was pursuing his abrasive path in Campobello, more positive developments were taking place on neighbouring islands and the mainland. Although the St Andrews peninsula and some of the islands had European inhabitants by 1775, extensive settlement had to await the resolution of the Revolutionary War. The defeat of the British had left stranded, and in danger of reprisals, tens of thousands of Americans who had remained loyal to the King. The Treaty of Paris (1783) guaranteed their safety and the restoration of their property and civic rights, but feelings against the Loyalists ran so high that the promises were impossible to keep. Flight was the only practical course and, for the great majority, Canada, or British North America, the only practical destination. About twenty-eight thousand moved to the province of Nova Scotia, slightly more than half of these settling on the north side of the Bay of Fundy in the area that would become the province of New Brunswick. The Quoddy region's share was roughly fifteen hundred.

Like most Loyalist groups the Passamaquoddy contingent was a mixture of civilians and soldiers, the latter from disbanded Loyalist regiments. Most of the soldiers were Royal Fencible Americans and Argyll Highlanders, the latter from the 74th Regiment. The civilians, who outnumbered them, were mostly members of the Penobscot Association, a group of merchants and professional men from Portland, Boston and New York who had sought the shelter of Fort George, a British stronghold adjacent to the town of Castine in what is now Maine. Castine lies on an isthmus at the point where the Penobscot River empties into the sheltered waters of Penobscot Bay. From Castine, the merchants continued to trade with Britain and the West Indies in the expectation that at the war's end the

Penobscot would divide the United States and British North America. More than this, they hoped for the creation of a new British colony, New Ireland, between the Penobscot and the St Croix. Lodged between New England and New Scotland, New Ireland would complete the imperial geography of the north-east coast.

But when the negotiators of the peace in Paris confounded their expectations by designating the St Croix as the international boundary, the Castine Loyalists found themselves still in enemy territory. They were forced to move again. In the summer of 1783, scouts were sent north to find a site from which they could continue to trade with the West Indies, and as if imprinted with the landscape of the lower Penobscot they settled for a sloping peninsular site at the point where the St Croix entered the protected waters of Passamaquoddy Bay. Conditions at Castine had virtually been duplicated. This new site had also been a principal camping ground for the Passamaquoddy Indians and a place where a French priest, Father St André, may have planted a cross. East of the peninsula, for a distance of thirty or forty miles, lay a rocky, inhospitable shore: a "belt of miserable spruce," in the eyes of the Scottish observer Patrick Campbell, "fit to be inhabited only by wild beasts."

To prepare for the arrival of the Loyalists, a townsite had to be surveyed and farm lots laid out along the river and around the shores of the Bay. The model for the survey was the New England township but the land divisions, as in old England, were called parishes not townships. Surveying began in mid August, 1783, and ended in late September. On October 3 two large transports and several smaller vessels bearing the first contingent of Loyalists sailed into Passamaquoddy Bay. In all, roughly a thousand would make the journey to St Andrews, about 650 civilians of the Penobscot Association and possibly two to three hundred discharged soldiers, fewer than half of whom had wives.

To avoid the chaos that had attended the arrival of the Loyalists in Saint John and Shelburne, lots were drawn before embarkation. Each family head was entitled to a town lot and a farm or "garden" lot of one hundred acres along the river or along the shores of the Bay. Town lots had to be built on within a year or be forfeited. Such was the commercial nature of the St Andrews settlement that of

The St Andrews peninsula. The Loyalists landed near the head of the wharf, in the right foreground.

the 430 grants issued more than three-quarters were for town lots only. Even so, only Loyalists of unquestioned fealty were granted choice river-front farmlands along the St Croix. Irish-born Americans from New Londonderry, New Hampshire, though declared Loyalists, were directed inland to St David's Parish. Although the soils of St David's were moderately fertile, lands back from the shore were generally regarded as "wild" lands, fit only for lumbering.

Inevitably, the first years were trying. Winters were hard and the tools, seeds, and equipment promised by the British were slow to arrive. Robert Pagan, one of the leaders, complained to the authorities of the "distressed and alarming situation of all the Inhabitants in this Bay;" and in 1784 a methodist minister from Halifax arrived to find numbers of civilians and soldiers living in bark huts and barely subsisting on government rations. But privation did not stunt the growth of the settlement. Within six months of the founding, William Pagan, brother to Robert, could write to a friend: "We have now about Ninety houses up, and great preparations making in every quarter of the Town for more. Numbers of Inhabitants are daily arriving and a great many others are hourly looked for from different quarters." By 1788 there were more than 250 houses in the town and well over a thousand people.

Deer Island ↷

THOUGH ST ANDREWS WAS THE FOCUS of Loyalist settlement in Passamaquoddy, there was movement onto adjacent shores and islands as well as into the hinterland. By 1785 the entire population of Passamaquoddy was almost two thousand. On Deer Island, as on Campobello, the path of settlement did not run smooth. In 1767 the island had been granted to a former British officer, Colonel Joseph William Gorham, and—after Gorham had been appointed Commandant of Newfoundland—sold in 1770 to Thomas Farrell, a Virginian.

As a proprietor, Farrell proved to be as intransigent as David Owen on Campobello. According to Martha Ford Barto, a Deer Island historian, Farrell made only trifling improvements to the island and made no effort to encourage or assist settlement. Reluctant to grant title to land, he insisted, wherever possible, on lease rather than sale. In his 1808 commentary on conditions in Passamaquoddy, Captain Nicolls was as dismissive of rentier conditions on Deer Island as on Campobello. He noted that the people of Deer Island were mostly fishermen living in small houses scattered along the shore and that settlement had been hindered by the "refusal" of the proprietor, Captain Farrell, to grant title deeds. In despair, some Loyalists moved to the mainland, some to Grand Manan, and some even back to the United States. To compound the irony, Farrell, who

Lord's Cove, Deer Island.

claimed to have once served in a British
regiment in the Revolutionary War, in
actuality supported the rebel side.

In 1812, the heads of twenty-two Deer Island families petitioned the
commander in chief of the Province of New Brunswick for title to two hundred
acre lots. The petitioners complained that after twenty years on the island, and
being still without title to their lands, they were afraid of being "dispossessed of
all" and "exposed to cold and hunger." They thought it "very hard" that Thomas
Farrell, who had been in the "American Service" during the Revolutionary War,
should have received extensive favours from Government when they themselves,
as staunch Loyalists, had been "totally disregarded." Even more galling, Farrell
had paid only half of the four hundred pounds promised to Colonel Gorham, the

original grantee, for title to the Island. When Farrell died in 1822, thirty-eight years after the arrival of the Loyalists, he still owned almost half of the land. Passamaquoddy may have been on the threshold of the New World but it was weighed down with the spirit of the Old.

GRAND MANAN ͻ

In contrast to Campobello and Deer Island, Grand Manan had no proprietor to obstruct the course of settlement. Fifteen miles long and, at its widest point, nearly seven across, it was by far the largest island of the archipelago. But fogbound and wet, and eighteen miles from the nearest point on the New Brunswick mainland and seven from Maine, it held no great attraction either for Indians or Europeans. To Maine, from which it is clearly visible, Grand Manan presents a line of towering cliffs. Indians occasionally paddled across to hunt porpoises and seals and collect feathers and gull, tern, and eider eggs, but they did not stay. Even their name for it is inconsequential. *Munanouk* means simply "island in the sea."

   When Captain Owen visited the island in August, 1770, he, too, was unimpressed even though he enjoyed shooting and battering the unsuspecting shorebirds. Owen, Captain Plato Denny, and the *Snow Owen's* pilot sailed from Campobello in the snow's longboat. At their first landfall—a salt marsh on the east coast near what is now the village of Castalia—they found an indifferent harbour that might, in a crisis, serve as a "tolerable asylum" for fishermen and small craft. In the channel between Ross and Cheney islands the longboat was left high and dry by the receding tide. Two summering Indians took them by canoe to the main island where they made a fire, boiled a teakettle, breakfasted, and shot more birds. At Grand Harbour they found the captain of a sloop, named *Hay Sloop,* and a party of men cutting hay for a patron in Gouldsboro, Maine. Even Grand Harbour, which Owen must have seen only at low tide, he was unable to recommend to vessels unless under "stress of weather, or real business." Seal Cove

he found less intimidating but still not attractive enough to delay his return to Campobello.

"Island in the Sea." Grand Manan's intimidating, cliff-bound west coast seen from Liberty Point, Campobello, seven miles away.

Only as a refuge was Grand Manan appealing. The first permanent settlers arrived after the Revolution in May 1784. Led by Moses Gerrish, a graduate of Harvard and a maker of counterfeit rebel bills in the late war, they were given license to occupy the island and, provided they could bring in fifty families within five years, the promise of title to the whole island. Isolation, fog, dangerous waters and a rugged coastline were, however, powerful deterrents, and at the end of the five years the licensees were well short of the fifty-family target. They themselves weathered the first seasons by hand-lining herring, shooting gulls and other seabirds, and sowing crops in the meagre soil.

Yet the population did grow. A survey conducted in 1805 to confirm or validate existing improvements, found more than fifty households scattered along the gentler and more sheltered east coast. Of the fifty-four lots surveyed, twenty-four were for "Emigrants from the United States," thirteen for Loyalists who had

taken temporary refuge elsewhere in British
territory, two for natives of Campobello, and
five for immigrants from Britain. Among

Moose Island, Maine, now connected to
the mainland by a causeway. In the
background is Cobscook Bay. The town
of Eastport is just off, to the left.

them, as described in the 1805 report, were Abner Meigs, who "Profess[ed] the
Practise of Physick," Josiah Flag, a native of Campobello and "a licensed pilot at St
Andrews," Thomas Dawkins, "a single man, a blacksmith," Josias Southwick, "a
useful settler and owner of a large schooner," John Hall "an Emigrant about 2
years hence from the United States ... [who] professes School Keeping," and
Henry Kimball "a British subject and an old soldier."

   Though the entire population in 1805 was only two hundred, the seeds of
future settlements had been planted. There were clusters of settlers at Flagg's
Cove (North Head) and Castalia. Woodward's Cove had a ship-building yard and
at Seal Cove which, according to the surveyor's report, "promised to be a very
regular and extensive settlement," an enterprising Yankee and noted physician, Dr
John Faxon, had bought a tract of land and divided it into lots which he
subsequently sold to Americans. In the Revolution Faxon had fought on the rebel

side. He opened the natural spit or sea wall that had closed Seal Cove harbour, and also built the only full rigged ship over five hundred tons ever launched from Grand Manan. But the outbreak of the 1812 War was too much for Dr Faxon's republican sympathies; he left the island, living afterwards at Lubec and Machias. Whitehead Island would soon be settled and Deep Cove would, for a time, outshine Seal Cove as a growing hamlet.

By 1818 there were seventy-one families on the island and a population of 384, with some two thousand acres under tillage. By 1824 the the population had reached six hundred, and by 1839 most of the usable coastal lots had been granted and occupied, and the wooded back lots staked out. Yet the population had grown not, as had been hoped, by the accretion of Loyalists, but, as the authors of the 1818 report noted, by the immigration of people "chiefly from the States" who were "strongly tinctured with American manners and principles." They had been attracted by its proximity to Maine and a persistent rumour, amounting to expectation, that the island would be ceded to Massachusetts.

In his *Journal* for 1811, Lieutenant Colonel Joseph Gubbins, Inspecting Field Officer of Militia, noted that the people of Grand Manan were not looked upon as staunch royalists. Confirmation of republican sympathies came from the island's first Anglican clergyman, the angst-ridden Cornelius Griffin, appointed in 1824. After noting that "the inhabitants are from the United States or connected therewith by marriage," Griffin dismissed them as "being of the lowest order & [like virtually everyone else in the islands] smugglers."

Moose Island ᴓ

Of the larger islands at the mouth of Passamaquoddy Bay, the only one not to fall into British or Loyalist hands was Moose Island, now Eastport. The island's first occupants were a handful of Nova Scotians who fished and cut lumber, and later served as a pretext for Britain's claims of sovereignty. The Treaty of Paris (1783) established the international boundary only as far as the mouth of the St

Croix. On his 1808 visit, Captain Nicolls, possibly with a prejudiced British eye, found Moose Island much less appealing than its New Brunswick neighbours: "Nature has been by no means lavish of her bounties to it, it produces little corn [and] no timber of any value." Yet with a fine, deep-water harbour and ready access to the Passamaquoddy fishing grounds, it proved attractive to Americans. Numbers of them moved in toward the end of the War of Independence and claimed it for the United States. By 1790 there were 240 people on the island and by 1800 twice this number.

Yet in spite of a strong American presence, there were periodic reminders from the British of the uncertain ownership of the island. Justices at St Andrews—the only settlement in the archipelago with established courts—attempted to bring it under their legislative wing by issuing warrants against Moose Islanders. In 1785, the sheriff of St Andrews crossed the Bay and arrested the Massachusetts collector of customs for charges of debt. The sheriff was forced to release him when he refused to recognize British authority; but the "Freetowners," as the Moose Islanders called themselves, naturally resented the presumption and in 1786 appealed to the Governor of Massachusetts for protection against unwanted warrants: "no allurements or threats," they vowed, "will prompt us to forsake that system and constitution which we hold as our natural right and privilege." When the island's population was large enough to warrant incorporation as a town, the Freetowners petitioned the Massachusetts Legislature, and the Legislature, ignoring lingering British claims to the island, passed a bill of incorporation in 1798. The bill admitted not Freetown, but "Eastport" into the Commonwealth of Massachusetts. The new name was thought to be more distinguished and, geographically speaking, more accurate.

MAKING A LIVING

SETTLERS IN St Andrews and the Bay islands turned automatically to the sea. The sea was their highway and, though few had been fishermen, it was also their most valuable resource. The Bay was rich in pollock, cod, hake, haddock and herring as well as lobster and scallops—the delicious shellfish. The land was heavily wooded but soils, on this glaciated northern end of the Appalachians, were thin, acid and stony. The climate, too, was cool and moist, and fogs were frequent. Spring—because of the coldness of Fundy waters—was invariably late and the growing season, for a region in the same latitude as Southern France, short.

Soils were deep enough to be worked only on the St Andrews peninsula and in patches on the islands. On the peninsula, as in parts of Scotland and Ireland, they were dressed with seaweed or "rockweed," and "mussel-mud"—mud filled with mussel shells from the Bay and some of the smaller inlets and creeks up the St Croix. Island and peninsula soils could sustain hay, oats and potatoes but with no major money crop, and only local markets for the staples, farming was marginal and usually had to be combined with fishing and winter work in the woods. No farm family could cultivate more than twelve or fifteen acres, even under the best of conditions. Other occupations returned more than farming, and once there was no longer a need for locally produced food, most farms were abandoned.

On the islands, where there were no surveys in advance of settlement, forests had to be cleared to provide land for cultivation or pasture. A typical holding consisted of a house, garden, pasture or "mowing-lot," and a field or two for oats, hay, and potatoes. Except for sheep-raising on the rich grasses of some of the islands, which were predator-free, there were no distinctive crops or husbandries. Grass, which likes cool, wet conditions, produced heavy crops of hay. The names of some of the smaller islands, such as Sheep Island and Hay Island off Grand Manan, attest to their function. At low water, sheep clambered onto the rocks to feed on seaweed nourishing enough, so their owners claimed, to keep them fat through the winter. Often there were no fences, the woods and the shore serving to pen the animals.

But as settlements grew, animals had to be tethered or confined, and in the Owen fiefdom of Campobello this gave rise to restrictions and offices with a curiously Old World ring. At the 1836 Sessions in Welshpool, it was decreed that no swine could run at large without being yoked or ringed, that wandering cattle, swine, sheep or goats were liable to capture and impoundment by "Hog Reeves" and "Pound Keepers," and that all fines levied were to be passed on to the "Overseers of the Poor."

In the merchant settlement of St Andrews, however, there was little interest in farming from the outset. Food could, if necessary, be imported. Matthew Lymburner, who arrived in 1784 with every intention of farming, left in 1785 having decided that St Andrews was a "sufficient accommodation for

Navy Island, which guards St Andrews harbour, was once settled, cleared, and farmed, but like most farmland in the Quoddy region it has since reverted to forest. The headstone, made from layered sandstone exposed on the shore, marks the grave of Joseph Meloney who died in 1821 at the age of forty-five. The white pine on the island was reserved for Royal Naval masts and spars.

artizans, but not for farming folk." Settlers were entitled to farm lots but many of the grantees were interested only in lumber and had no intention of breaking the ground. Traders and merchants had eyes only for the lucrative West Indian trade and their chief aim was to corner the market by eliminating American competition. To do this required that Great Britain enforce her navigation laws.

These laid down that, barring emergencies, goods for British or imperial markets must be carried in British vessels. But first, Loyalist traders and merchants had to convince officials in London, who knew next to nothing of the geography of North America, that the British colonies could provide the West Indian planters with all the fish, lumber, and naval stores they needed.

Confident assertions were the order of the day. Edward Winslow declared that he was "perfectly satisfied" that Nova Scotia and Canada had more than enough lumber, water power and labour to satisfy every West Indian need. Even more optimistic was William Pagan of St Andrews who saw no need to involve the rest of Canada. Except for oak staves, which were used to make barrels, he thought "the Grand Bay of Passamaquoddy alone [could] supply the whole British West India Islands with Boards, Planks, Scantling, Ranging Timber, Shingles, [and] Clapboards." Masts, spars, and square timber for the British market, he noted prophetically, were only limited by "the want of Inhabitants and Saw mills."

Pagan seemed as good as his word. By the end of May, 1785, barely seven months after their arrival, the Penobscot Loyalists had sent off their first cargoes of lumber and fish. Rum (still the region's favourite tipple), molasses, sugar and salt were the return cargoes. According to John Springer, an early historian of lumbering, in the winter of 1832 between 450 and 550 Maine and New Brunswick woodsmen drank 15,900 litres (about 3,500 gallons) of "ardent spirits." These, along with molasses and sugar, could be bought in any store displaying the sign "W-I" Goods. Molasses, so it has been said, sweetened the wilderness and energized the lumbermen. Patrick Campbell, a Scots emissary who had been sent out to determine whether Canada might make a suitable home for Highlanders, noted in 1793 that the new town of St Andrews, "prettily situated, on a spacious point of land, with an easy slope towards the water," had "a smart trade in ship building, lumber, and fish." He also predicted, all too accurately, that the pretty situation would last longer than the trade.

Mac Armstrong's water-driven sawmill, near St Andrews: a lone survival from the days of "wood, wind and water."

LUMBERING ✍

THOUGH PROFITABLE, the West Indies lumber
trade merely scratched the forests of the St Croix. Much of the wood, in any case,
was cut on the American side, and brought to New Brunswick ports for
shipment. The real test of the resource had to await a new round in hostilities
between England and France. To avenge his defeat at Trafalgar, Napoleon, in
1807, persuaded the Russian Emperor, Alexander I, to close the Baltic to British
ships: Norway, Sweden, and the Baltic countries were Britain's chief sources of
lumber. In that same year, President Jefferson imposed an embargo on overseas
trade, thereby cutting off British supplies of American lumber. As lumber prices
in Britain soared, and duties against colonial timber toppled, axes were taken

down and sharpened along the Miramichi, the St John, and the St Croix. Around the shores of the Bay and on the islands, hundreds of farmer-fishermen put up their oars and stored their nets to move upriver to St Stephen, the bridgehead for the assault on the forests of the St Croix.

Cutting was reckless. The lumbermen were interested chiefly in white pine and each harvested tree was expected to yield a thousand board-feet of plank or a piece of ton-timber at least a foot square. In felling and hauling out the massive "sticks" of pine, some six feet across at the base and 150 feet long, smaller trees were destroyed. Ideas of conservation were still in their infancy and even though George Perkins Marsh, the father of the modern conservation movement, was a Vermonter, it is unlikely that counsels of restraint reached the St Croix. Even so, Captain Joseph Hatch, assistant deputy surveyor of the King's Woods for Charlotte County, was thoroughly shaken by the cutting. He complained in 1809 of the great wastage of timber, of the overnight doubling of output, and of the woods as a bonanza that absorbed, in winter, "seventeen twentieths" of the manpower of the county.

Lumbering also made inroads into farming and family life. In theory, winter work in the woods and summer work on the farm ought to have complemented each other, but work in the woods usually ran into the spring, sometimes delaying planting and shortening the season. Young men, too, as the *Calais Advertiser* noted, who had tasted the camaraderie and shared work of a lumber camp had no relish for picking up stones alone on a ten-acre plot. And there was, in any case, little incentive to farm when a few days work on a boom or at a millpond could buy a barrel of American flour.

Family life suffered from the long absences and from the heavy drinking that accompanied camp life. Yet for the settler with no cash and no means of getting credit, winter work in the woods was a lifeline. Lumbering underwrote many a farm but the trade got a consistently bad press. According to prevailing views of political economy, farming was the only sure foundation for growth.

SHIPBUILDING ↝

THE BITE OF THE AXE may have been the true symphony of the St Croix, but along the tidewater reaches and out in the Bay it synchronized with the ring of the hammer and the thud of the caulking mall. The cheapest way of getting lumber to British markets was to build vessels to carry it, and at the end of the voyage sell both cargo and carrier. So began the synergy of mutually reinforcing industries that brought vigour to the Maritime economy. Ships' timber lay close to the shore and any flat, sheltered site close to a town or village was a potential shipyard. There were yards in St Andrews and St Stephen and in all the major harbours on the islands.

Yards in Calais, Robbinston, Eastport and Lubec were equally busy, but not with ships for the British trade. On outgoing tides the St Croix was often

Sodom Cove, Eastport. In sheltered coves and inlets such as this, boats were built in most of the settlements of the Quoddy region. In the background is the island of Campobello. On dark or foggy nights, coves like Sodom were also havens for smugglers. In the foreground are lupines, floral emblems of the region and behind them, near the water, is yet another regional icon: an abandoned boat.

The remains of an old wet-dock or float in Chamcook Harbour, near St Andrews.
The wooden dam (built in the 1820s) contained the flood tide water, thus sparing
vessels loading and unloading from having to "take the ground" at the ebb.
Reinforced with modern netting, it now serves as a weir used by the Atlantic
Salmon Federation for trapping salmon returning to the Chamcook stream.
Around the harbour, ships were built for Chamcook's thriving lumber trade.

white with sail as merchantmen, fishing vessels, and even whalers made for Great Britain, the West Indies, the Grand Banks, and the South Pacific. Waterfronts were lined with wharves, ships, warehouses, and chandleries, and the men who manned or frequented them were often more familiar with Liverpool and Havana than with towns up and down the Maine or New Brunswick coasts. Children then, as some archival records remind us, were adept at naming types of vessels as later ones were with types of automobiles and aeroplanes.

Local lore has it that the shore of the St Andrews peninsula was once so thick with wharves and moored vessels that an agile walker could wharf-and-deck hop from Joe's Point to the end of the peninsula, a distance of about a mile, without wetting his feet. Today, apart from the town wharf (in the background), only a few rotting stumps remain.

But quantity of shipbuilding was, of course, no guarantee of quality. In shipping circles, New Brunswick yards had a poor reputation until the middle of the 19th century. With no reservoir of skill, and protected by the navigation laws from competition with yards in Maine, they built only to the minimum standards; lower timbers were of pine or spruce instead of the traditional oak and they were seldom seasoned. Built for speculations on the open market—rather than being commissioned—the vessels were not properly finished. On arrival in Britain after a rough North Atlantic passage some were barely seaworthy. Shipbuilders described them as "patched together" or "slop" or "cabbage built"; seamen as "softwood ships," "leather ships" and "sailors coffins." Lloyds gave them a low rating and in 1849 installed a London surveyor in New Brunswick to supervise the building of large vessels.

For every yard building vessels for the trans-Atlantic trade and the deep sea or offshore fishery, there were a dozen others making small craft for fishing inshore. In winter many a fish stand became a small boat shop where a vessel was built for the next season. If the intended boat happened to be too big for the shop, building operations were simply moved to the nearest field. The most common of the inshore fishing boats, a "pinky" or "Quoddy pink," was pointed or "pinked" at both ends and, because it carried a large sail, it was also deep-draughted. Unlike boats with transoms, boats with two pointed ends, "pea pods," were relatively easy to build, prow and stern being framed in exactly the same way.

THE CARRYING TRADE ↪

As SUPPLIERS OF FOOD AND RAW MATERIALS to Great Britain and the West Indies, Nova Scotia and New Brunswick were no substitute for the American colonies. Both provinces had fish, and New Brunswick had lumber, but in addition to fish and lumber the "Sugar Islands" needed biscuit and flour, corn and meal, pork, beef, butter and cheese, and New Brunswick and Nova Scotia were in no position to supply them. Fishing, trading, lumbering, and shipbuilding were so much more profitable than farming that most people were even reluctant, as Governor Parr remarked resignedly, to set aside enough time to "raise themselves a little bread." When a barrel of mackerel would buy two of flour only a dedicated husbandman would exchange handlines for a plough. Both provinces imported large quantities of flour and meat from New England.

Pieces of flint and coral, the 150 year-old remains of ballast carried in vessels returning from England and the West Indies can still be found in St Andrews harbour. The corral is the the large white rock in the foreground, the flint the much smaller taffy-coloured piece to the left.

In spite of the failure of the Maritimes to live up to their claims of being potential cornucopia, neither the British West Indies nor Great Britain wanted for provisions. Commerce, like nature, abhors a vacuum. To supply British and West Indian markets, Americans either defied the navigation laws or circumvented them. When Horatio Nelson was sent to Barbados in 1786 to enforce the laws he found so many American flags that he had to remind himself that he was in British territory: "Had I been set down from the air I should most assuredly have been convinced that I was in an American instead of a British port." To circumvent the Navigation Laws, Americans simply transferred their flour and other foodstuffs to British vessels or "bottoms." Trading on "the Lines," that is rendezvousing with American ships for the exchange of goods in waters over which neither Britain nor the United States had jurisdiction, became a way of life for Passamaquoddy merchants and shipowners.

But even more profitable for local carriers than prohibitive shipping laws were outright hostilities between the Atlantic powers. The renewal, in 1803, of the protracted war between England and France had immediate repercussions in Passamaquoddy Bay. British efforts to cut off trade between France and the neutral powers led to the search and seizure of American vessels and impressment of their crews. To prevent the harassment, President Jefferson, in 1807, imposed an embargo on all overseas trade and, as a safeguard against even greater aggression, he began making plans for a system of coastal defences.

Along the eastern seaboard, where no American vessel could clear for a foreign port, overseas trade came to a standstill except in ports close to the Lines. Overnight, Eastport became the busiest port in the Union. Within a ten-minute boat ride of the British islands, and a Swiss cheese of secluded coves and inlets, it was a conduit for flour, salted meat and naval stores shipped up the coast from the middle and southern states and then ferried across the Lines to Campobello, Indian Island, St Andrews and Saint John. More goods crossed at Robbinston and other secluded points along the coast. Passamaquoddy Bay swarmed with American craft of all sizes, many of which, under pretence of needing repairs, put into port with flour and fish. On the Canadian side, American carriers picked up

Eastport waterfront from Campobello, seen through the tracery of an old herring weir.

manufactured goods shipped directly to St Andrews by merchants in Liverpool. Manufacturing in the United States was still in its infancy.

As the focus of the illicit traffic, Eastport became, in the American historian Lorenzo Sabine's memorable phrase, a "citadel for the smuggling gentry." Adventurers, debtors, and deserters from the British army and the British navy descended on the island swelling the "band of Yanky smugglers" that the loyal Scotsman Patrick Campbell had found there on his visit in 1793. So urgent were the currents of trade that the federal government was powerless to stop them. At any one time as many as a dozen vessels, some bearing tauntingly appropriate names, such as *Honest Tom, The Federal, Hazard, The Mindwell* and

The Financier, lay in Eastport harbour waiting to unload. Wharves groaned under their burdens of barreled flour, beef and pork, and sheds and warehouses were filled to overflowing. Surpluses were piled high on the beaches at Eastport and Robbinston for shipment to Campobello, Indian Island and St Andrews, and between West Quoddy Head and the Machias River for shipment to Grand Manan. All the piles were in full view of the few federal gunboats in the Bay, and of the sentries supplied by the garrison at Fort Sullivan or hired by the collector of customs, but still they dwindled. As almost every observer remarked, to keep flour in Eastport at four dollars a barrel when two miles away the same barrel fetched twelve dollars was asking too much of human nature.

The sentries, who were mostly underpaid and ill-equipped deserters from the British army, were eminently bribeable. For a price, payable either in cash or liquor, they allowed the smugglers to carry off as much flour and salt meat as they pleased. Guards and informers could also be distracted. Two associations of smugglers, the "Jew's Harp" and "Dandelion" societies, are said to have played and danced in public places while their colleagues smuggled. In a well-known sketch, each of the performers was shown with a jew's harp while about a dozen people encircled a table, each holding a salt fish that was supposed to represent a music book.

Federal gunboats were a more serious obstacle than venal sentries but there were few of them, and in fog and darkness small vessels, boats and even canoes handled by men acquainted with every cove, inlet and current were difficult to detect. Eastport and Campobello men used to say covertly that they knew why fogs were made. There were occasional skirmishes with revenuers but the prizes made the risks worthwhile. Once across the Lines the carriers were picked up by armed British sloops and escorted to safe landings in St Andrews or the islands.

Not even the War of 1812 between Britain and the United States had any lasting effect on the flow of trans-Atlantic traffic. There was an immediate slowdown as trading across the Lines became, technically speaking, the crime of aiding and abetting the enemy but it quickly resumed its pre-war proportions. In

New Brunswick and Massachusetts (which then encompassed Maine) there was no enthusiasm for the war and no earnest pursuit of the miscreants. The Governor of Massachusetts refused to allow any section of the militia to march out of the state and it was rumoured that American vessels in Boston harbour, on hearing of the declaration of war, put their flags at half mast. In southern New Brunswick and northern Maine, communities on opposite sides of the border vowed never to take up arms against the other, and the carriers among them had no intention of letting a war that had been foisted on them by bellicose leaders decimate their profits.

Normal traffic quickly resumed. Moose Islanders, observed Collector Elkanah Morton of Halifax—and he could well have added Indian Islanders or Grand Mananers—were "much more disposed for smuggling than war." No strangers to euphemism, Moose Islanders described their position as a wish to continue "an amicable intercourse." Governor Sherbrooke of Nova Scotia, who was also impressed by the "friendly disposition" manifested by the supposedly warring states, reported (in August 1812) that the demand for British manufactures had led various enterprising American traders to attempt evasion of their own laws.

On the British side, the demand for American grain, flour, lumber, pitch, tar and turpentine reached such levels that a licensing system was organized allowing American vessels access to Maritime ports. In New Brunswick trading with the enemy became a patriotic duty and in the unlikely event of being apprehended many merchant vessels carried fake foreign registries (usually Norwegian or Swedish) so that they could pose as neutrals. Many a Maine vessel, too, papers all in order for delivery within the United States, would get blown off course and with compass conveniently out of kilter be forced to take refuge in a West Indian port.

Eastport again became a conduit for trans-Atlantic traffic when the British, in 1814, announced a blockade of the entire Atlantic coast. Though impossible to enforce, the mere threat of it was enough to intensify flows through Eastport. Bales and casks of manufactured silk, wool, cotton and

In its heyday as an entrepot for the West Indian trade, Indian Island had a population large enough to support a small school. The shore was lined with houses, wharves and storage sheds. Now only the ruins of a few houses and the stumps of wharves remain. In the background, to the far left, is Moose Island, about a mile away.

metals from Britain and the West Indies were stored in sheds and warehouses on Indian Island and Campobello, and at night shipped across the Lines in "neutral" vessels. Indian Island, which is now uninhabited, was then a vital entrepot with a resident population of about 250, large enough to support a small school. Along its waterfront were wharves and warehouses, and berthing places for several large vessels.

Once safely across the Lines, the goods were moved by boat up the streams and bays and then transferred to horse-drawn wagons for shipment to Portland, Boston, and New York. Known as the fleet of "mud clippers" or the "Horse Marine," the lumbering four-horse teams were the butt of many a sea-farer's joke.

Although most officials clearly connived at the illegal traffic, others were outraged by it. Prominent among the latter was the unbending and unpopular

The view across the Lines from Fort Sullivan, Eastport.

Major-General George Ulmer, commander of the garrison
at Eastport from 1812. Aghast to discover that almost half
of the town's more than two hundred merchants and traders were British subjects
engaged in illicit trade with New Brunswick, he gave the interlopers six days to
swear an oath of loyalty to the United States on pain of returning to New
Brunswick or becoming prisoners of war. Three-quarters of them took the oath,
but, on hearing of the decree, officials in Washington, who were attuned to New
England sentiments, ordered Ulmer to rescind it and simply enforce existing laws.

      Ulmer's appeals for federal gun-boats to police the illicit traffic and
restrain British warships in the Bay proved equally fruitless. From his eyrie at Fort
Sullivan, Ulmer had a grandstand view of the harbour and the Bay. Unable to fire
even warning shots, he was forced to watch direct exchanges between American
and British vessels and "seizures" of laden American vessels by British warships.
The seizures he knew to be nothing more than abductions arranged for the
shippers by local agents. The American owners followed the seized vessels to
Saint John or Halifax and pretended to ransom them when, in effect, they were

being paid for their cargoes. Other owners arranged to have British privateers take their vessels to St Andrews where, as in Saint John and Halifax, they were allowed to sell the cargoes and then "ransom" their vessels. Returning vessels often called at Campobello or Indian Island with loads of plaster or grindstones for smuggling in due season to Eastport.

A war in which, Ulmer complained bitterly to his superiors, "every plan that can be devised is taken to supply the enemy with provisions" was more than he could comprehend or tolerate. To maintain his poorly provisioned and—for months at a time—unpaid command, Ulmer went very heavily into debt. Unable to meet his creditors, he was arrested by the local sheriff and held for two weeks in the county gaol in Machias. Vilified by Moose Islanders and the target of vicious rumours, he was finally—after a biased army inquiry—relieved of his command and placed under arrest. No formal charges were ever laid against him but until his enlistment ran out some months later he languished in prison.

Ulmer's successor as commander of the garrison at Eastport, Major Perley Putnum, was equally unsuccessful in his efforts to control the illegal trans-Atlantic traffic. Shortly after his arrival, in March 1814, he ignored federal government instructions and ordered a shot fired across the bow of an Eastport schooner seen crossing into British waters. The schooner may have broken a law by crossing the Lines but by firing the shot, Putnum had crossed a rubicon. The town rose against the garrison, evincing such open hostility that for two-and-a-half months—until relieved by the British capture of the island—officers and men lived under a state of virtual seige. Officers billeted in the town were given notice to leave and the men, who were not safe outside the pickets of the fort, were confined to barracks. Refused supplies by local merchants, they were also forced to live on government rations.

Eastport occupied ᘐ

THOUGH THE NEED TO MAINTAIN access to American foodstuffs and naval stores determined British strategy in Passamaquoddy Bay, the British had never ceased to covet Eastport itself. Moose Island was the one piece in the Passamaquoddy jigsaw that lay between them and complete control of the Bay. In official documents they invariably referred to Eastport as Moose Island, pointedly ignoring the American nomenclature. The direction taken by the international boundary after leaving the mouth of the St Croix still had to be ratified even though British and American negotiators had agreed, in 1803, that Deer Island, Indian Island and Campobello should remain British, and Moose, Frederick and Dudley Islands, American. Articles of convention had been prepared but never signed because of a disagreement between Britain and the United States over disputed territory in the upper Mississippi.

But with the ownership of Moose Island still not officially settled by the War of 1812, the British judged that occupation might decide the issue. In July 1814, five months before the end of the war, a British squadron sailed into Eastport harbour and for the next four years several hundred redcoated troops, some with families, occupied the island. Eastport's extended Fourth of July celebrations date from June 30, 1818, the last day of British rule. David Owen, who during the occupation lost a number of sheep to British "jacktars and lobsterjacks," insisted that he could have taken the town with a gun, a brig, and his own militia.

The British built a school, established a theatre group, held balls, and introduced horse racing, but rule was still military. Residents who stayed were required to take the oath of allegiance to the crown on the understanding, conveyed verbally by commander Sir Thomas Hardy of Trafalgar fame, that it was to be regarded as an oath of neutrality while they remained under British jurisdiction, not an avowal of perpetual allegiance. Taking him at his word, Eastporters voted in the election for governor of Massachusetts in 1816. But some

The ruins of the Fort Sullivan powder
magazine built by the British during the
occupation of 1814-1818.

were wary of British blandishments, among
them a wife and husband who, to spare their
child the ignominy of being born under even a temporary British flag, made a
canopy from the stars and stripes in the birthing room.

Houses and public buildings were commandeered for military use and
no one could leave town without a pass from the town major. The British also
seized goods in bonded warehouses, destined for the United States, and
demanded that their owners pay British as well as American duties. But double
duty was a penalty no self-respecting Eastport merchant could contemplate and
no fair-minded British officer impose. On hearing that the marshal of Nova
Scotia—who had been authorized to collect the duties—was arriving,
sympathetic officers gave fair warning to the merchants affected: the aptly named
Jabez Mowry, Ezra Buckram, Josiah Dana, Samuel Wheeler and Jonathan Bartlett.
That night, they loaded their goods into dories and stole across Broad Cove to

Flagg's Point. Storesheds and dwellings soon appeared on the wharves of the point, becoming, in Sumner Pike's phrase, "the nice little town at the Narrows of Lubec."

Though the British occupation eliminated smuggling across the Lines, Eastport's role as a smuggling citadel was far from over. The United States still needed British manufactures and the town and garrison were a natural market for the farmers of Maine who were not about to let US border guards prevent them from turning a handsome profit on beef, pork and poultry. From Eastport, British manufactures still flowed freely into the United States. "Neutral" vessels, equipped with foreign registries, crossed the cove to Lubec or sailed

Lying in some foreign field. The graves of two English officers, newly decorated with Union Jacks, who died during the occupation of Eastport, 175 years ago.

down the coast to Hampden, a small port across the Penobscot from British-occupied Castine. The sloop *Abbo,* owned by a New Brunswicker living in Eastport, was notorious for the speed with which it could complete voyages from Sweden or Spain. The sloop changed flags and masters at will, and even when loaded to the water line and propelled by oars, it could—if the traffic warranted—make two "trans-Atlantic" voyages a day.

For the US collector of customs at Lubec, Major Lemuel Trescott, a veteran of the Revolutionary War who had overseen the construction of Fort Sullivan, life on a legal quicksand was as agonizing as it had been for Colonel Ulmer at Fort Sullivan. Trescott allowed the "neutral" traffic only because, as he noted despairingly, "the *law* overruled [him]." In a letter to the comptroller of the treasury, written in October 1814, he complained bitterly of his emasculation and suggested, since the British controlled every port from the Passamaquoddy to the Penobscot, that he might as well withdraw to Portland or some town west of it. Evidently hoping for a new posting, he left the district shortly after his declaration but in March of the following year he was back, clearly against his will. In a letter to General Dearborn at Boston he sighed: "God knows I have wished to avoid doing business at my office."

CONTRABAND ൭

IN ADDITION TO THE TRANS-ATLANTIC TRADE there was also a great deal of local smuggling; illegal movements of tea, cotton and tobacco far exceeded the legal traffic. The chief carriers were fishermen. Fishing boats could move freely within British and American waters and there were so many of them that only token surveillance was possible. Often, too, there was nothing in the manners, dress or speech of the owners—all spoke in the broad accents of the Bay—to denote their nationality. And to make surveillance even more difficult, British authorities had no automatic right to search and inspect American fishing vessels in Canadian waters. Under pretence of landing salt or provisions for their own use, Americans supplied New Brunswick and Nova Scotia with enough tea, rum, sugar, molasses, and wine to satisfy even the sweetest provincial tooth or the most demanding palate.

The other great pipeline for smuggled goods was the gypsum or plaster trade. The chief source of gypsum was at the head of the Bay of Fundy where New Brunswick and Nova Scotia meet, and the chief market the farms of the middle and southern seaboard states. Continuous cropping of wheat and tobacco had impoverished southern soils, and to maintain yields, farmers had to fertilize. Rich in calcium, gypsum, or plaster of Paris, was both a valuable natural fertilizer and a binding agent for structurally-weakened soils. To avoid the duties and stiff tonnage fees demanded of British vessels by American ports, carriers shipped the dirty-grey masses of gypsum to Campobello, the hub of the trade, where it could be picked up by New England coasters and taken to Boston, New York, Philadelphia, Baltimore or Charleston. Other vessels sidled across the Lines, (making a direct transfer) to American vessels anchored in quiet coves. During the summer months at the height of the trade, fifty to seventy American vessels might have lurked in the Bay waiting to take on cargoes.

On Campobello where there was no regular customs establishment—merely a deputy with a permanently blind eye—a hundred tons of plaster were landed in 1794, 14,000 tons in 1802. Smuggling was encouraged by David Owen who contended that the conditions of his grant exempted him from New Brunswick law. On their return journeys the gypsum boats were laden with flour, teas, coarse cottons, spirits, shoes and boots, and other contraband. Usually under thirty tons, the boats could coast along the shores in waters too shallow for the revenue boats, and land their cargoes in uninhabited bays and inlets. Smaller boats then picked up the cargoes, bore them up the rivers and inlets, and distributed them to every part of the country. "To such lengths has this trade been carried," noted a dejected Nova Scotia merchant, "that you can scarce enter a House, but you see an American package."

Policing the traffic was beyond even the powers of George Leonard, New Brunswick's zealous superintendent of trade and fisheries. A devout Loyalist,

Eastport (formerly "Freetown" and until 1818 never safe from British take-over) remains defiantly American. In this south end house, Old Glory replaces drapes.

Leonard regarded smuggling by Americans as simply a continuation of the Revolutionary War by other means. His first target as superintendent of trade was the illicit trade of the Passamaquoddy islands. In 1805, ignoring existing treaties amd agreements, he seized in Snug Cove, Campobello, an American sloop engaged in "smuggling." The owner appealed against the seizure on the grounds that sovereignty over the islands had not been officially decided and that the seizure contravened an informal arrangement between New Brunswick and American customs officials that plaster boats not be molested. To muddy the waters even further, the agent for the American owner was the surveyor and searcher of the Customs House at St Andrews, Colin Campbell, and the owner of the cargo in question none other than Campbell's son. Leonard's seizure caused so much consternation in so many official places that the British ambassador in Washington, Anthony Merry, in a letter to London expressed his incredulity at Leonard's conduct. Although a colonial court—the Court of the Vice Admiralty at Saint John—upheld Leonard's action, he received a note from Gabriel Ludlow, president of the provincial council, advising him to desist from further seizures.

The extent of smuggling, and the strong feelings that zealous suppression of it aroused, suggests an unusual degree of lawlessness in communities along the river and around the Bay. But the fault lay not with the nature of the people but with the nature of government. While admitting the necessity for exchange, both British and American governments placed difficulties—in the form of navigation laws, embargoes, and gratuitous wars—in the way of it. In the case of the trans-Atlantic and West Indian trade, local carriers were merely go-betweens: storers, shippers, and forwarders of the merchandise. The projectors, the great movers of the trade, were in England, the West Indies or on the eastern seaboard. In Passamaquoddy itself the legal machinery of prevention worked against, as the historian Gerald Graham remarked, "the insuperable opposition of geography and human nature." To impose trade restrictions in a neighbourhood of islands and peninsulas bound by ties of commerce, family, and friendship, and surrounded by fog-bound, difficult waters was, in effect, to invite larceny.

Even after the official division of the islands in 1817, jurisdiction over some of the smaller ones was still so uncertain that smugglers, when apprehended, could claim either British or American nationality. In some cases there was genuine duality. Many New Brunswickers had been born in the States and most of those living in Passamaquoddy had family ties in Maine. So close were Grand Manan's links with Maine that a quarter of a century after its official surrender to New Brunswick (in 1817) the American diplomat Daniel Webster could still regret the decision. Virtually all of Grand Manan's commerce was with Eastport and Lubec and many of the islanders were Americans with republican sympathies. The island had no resident customs officer until 1867 and no regular mail and passenger boat until 1884. Loyalties understandably were uncertain.

John Dunn, then sheriff of Charlotte County, despaired of ever being "able to make these fellows *good* British subjects."

In such convoluted political and legal waters, customs officials were tolerated only for as long as they remained in tune with local sensibilities. Officiousness was abhorred. In 1831, the merchants of St Andrews were so enraged by Collector Spearman's tiresome enforcement of the customs regulations that they petitioned the provincial legislative assembly for his removal. A lawsuit and a five day trial ensued in which Spearman was awarded one shilling for damages. Informers were liked even less than officious revenuers and were pilloried when discovered. An 1833 correspondent to the *St. Croix Courier* warned his neighbours to beware of a certain John G. . . . whom he had reason to believe was a customs informer and "a great scoundrel. We are all," he added affectingly, "in the habit of smuggling at different times." At Eastport, informing and officiousness were tolerated even less. Informers were tarred and feathered and on at least one occasion, a customs officer who had acted on a tip from an informer was tumbled into the dock. From time to time, too, local newspapers spoke out against customs regulations. Angered by what it considered to be an outbreak of officiousnes, the *Calais Gazette and Advertiser*, in July 1837, made a spirited defence of a free and open system: "The trade on this river has been conducted for thirty years on terms of perfect reciprocity. Owing to our peculiar situation there is no such thing as enforcing the letter of our revenue laws .... [By] the universal consent of our citizens and the tacit agreement of both governments, our trade has been wisely suffered to take its own course without interruption. Indeed it must ever be so, or *it must cease to exist.*"

Official observers, too, in a milieu where even the fastidiously law-abiding looked upon smuggling as part of normal intercourse, could be equally sympathetic. George Leonard Jr, who conducted an investigation of smuggling for the British Government early in the 19th century, concluded that the only place for the upright man with ambition lay far away from the siren shores of the Bay of Fundy. Thirty years later, Captain John Robb, commander of the sloop *Satellite*, came to much the same conclusion in his 1840 report on the state of the

Sumner Pike's "nice little town at the Narrows of Lubec."

fisheries and the contraband trade in the Bay of Fundy. The British government was particularly disturbed by the return traffic of flour, tea, tobacco, and spirits from Maine ports on local fishing vessels and the few remaining plaster boats from Nova Scotia.

Instead of deploring the traffic and castigating the traffickers, Robb argued for the repeal of laws that were impossible to enforce and that did harm by framing as illegal, and even immoral, behaviour that was driven as much by economic necessity as the desire to escape duties and tonnage fees. People in a province where there was little farming or manufacturing, observed Robb, "generally consider they commit no fraud by the infraction of a law, which they believe to be more honored in the breach than the observance." Even the crews of Her Majesty's ships assigned to police traffic in the Bay of Fundy had no stomach for work that was both ineffective and unjust. Robb noted that desertions were frequent whenever boats, lowered to apprehend smugglers, were detached from the ships for any length of time.

Robb's sentiments on smuggling were repeated almost to the letter a decade later by Isaac Woodward, Saint John's representative in the New Brunswick House of Assembly. In 1850, Woodward, a prominent shipper and importer, argued before the assembly that because trade between Grand Manan and Maine was both natural and necessary, the imposition of duties, which were impossible to collect, simply made that trade illicit. He moved—but to no purpose—that the duties be dropped. A petition with 120 signatories, "praying the Island may be established as a free Port," followed Woodward's failed motion and when it, too, failed to move the assembly, the petitioners extended the appeal to include the Deer Island and Campobello. A nervous assembly, however, rejected it on the grounds that it would increase smuggling from Grand Manan and Passamaquoddy to other parts of the province.

THE FISHERY ა

BY FAR THE MOST DURABLE OF THE PASSAMAQUODDY trades, if neither the most profitable nor the most exciting, was fishing. When the engaging and versatile Moses Perley conducted his survey of the fishery for the New Brunswick Legislature in 1850, he found that most of the Bay islanders were fishermen: industrious, hardy, hospitable and "peculiar in their manners," by which he meant nothing more serious than that they spoke a dialect conditioned, like all dialects, by environment and work. Their boots were "stampers," their aprons "barvels," their hats "sou'westers," their knives "throaters," and the boxes into which they threw the fish, "kids." They measured time not by the position of the sun or the hands of a watch but by the state of the tides; thus this morning at dawn and last night at dusk might be rendered as "this morning about low water slack" and "t'other night about half flood."

Fish were taken in a variety of ways. Near the shore, where most of the fishing was done, the simplest method was to handline them with a hook baited with fresh herring. Most ground fish—pollock, cod, hake and haddock—were caught in this way. At favoured fishing grounds such as the Big Eddy near Indian Island, two to three hundred small craft from both sides of the line might congregate at the "slacks" of the tide, i.e., just before high or low water. To avoid fouling the fishing lines, a minimum of anchors were dropped, the boats making fast to each other stem to stern and with just enough space between them to haul in the fish. There were usually two or three men to a boat, each hauling in their catches and exchanging jibes and banter with neighbouring boats. This "very gay" scene, noted an appreciative Moses Perley, was broken up only when the tide began to run, steering both fish and boats through the passages between the islands.

Hibernia weir, Deer Island. As herring move inshore to feed with the rising flood tide, the projecting "wing" of the weir diverts them into its nearly enclosed centre. In a good year a weir might take 2,000 hogsheads of herring (one hogshead is equal to 1,240 lbs) but in a bad year many weirs take nothing.

After 1850, Maine fishermen began using longlines or groundlines, anchored near the bottom, to which many short sections of line, each with a hook, were fastened. By increasing the catch, the long line encouraged fishing from larger vessels or, more accurately from dories attached to a mother vessel, usually a schooner. The versatile, flat bottomed dory handled well on the water, could be pulled up easily onto the beach, and nestled in stacks on the deck of the schooner.

Herring, the smallest and most numerous of the fish, were trapped or netted. At spawning time, adult herrings approach the shore and lay their eggs, about 30,000 per fish, in places where the young will be safe from deep-water predators. The richest spawning ground was off the southwest head of Grand Manan and until placed off-limits to fishing in 1851, four to five miles of nets tended by as many as a hundred vessels from both sides of the line, ringed the southern end of the island. Herring spawn was so thick that it washed up ankle deep on the beaches and encased nets, ropes and moorings: a slender rat line could grow to the thickness of a man's arm and a mooring to the girth of a five gallon keg.

In the fall and winter months, herring shoals, which tend to gather in river mouths and harbours, were also "driven" by fleets of small boats. Driving was a night operation. Herring are attracted by light and a fleet of small boats, each with a flare of birch bark or oil-soaked cotton batten suspended from a "devil" over the forward quarter of the boat, could set an entire shoal in motion. The secret of success was to keep the boats just ahead of the shoal, by rowing furiously, and dip into its leading edge with a broad net. The netted herring were rolled over into the bottom of the boat. Pollock, which are both bottom and surface feeders, were also dip-netted in this way, but during daylight and without the aid of flares.

But the most ingenious method of catching herring, and the most decorous, was to trap them in weirs. Europeans appear to have been using weirs by the end of the 18th century, but the conception of a fish weir is undoubtedly Indian. The Passamaquoddy and Fundy weirs, which are still very much in use,

Fishing gear at Woodward's Cove, Grand Manan: in the foreground modern scallop drags and net buoys, and in the background boat sheds and old smoke houses.

are sinuous arrangements of poles and nets that shore-hugging shoals of herring readily find their way into but, because the trap curls inward on itself, cannot easily find their way out. Weirs are usually set at the extreme end of some point of land or in channels between islands or ledges where herring are known to run. Most are arranged so that the mouth opening is toward the west, the best catches being in the early morning when, so it is said, the herring, attracted by the light, are moving toward the sun.

Weirs were made of upright poles driven into the mud, or, if the bottom was hard and the fish runs heavy enough to warrant the labour, anchored with rocks. To trap herring now, the poles—usually birch saplings—are hung with fine nylon netting but the first coverings were of woven brush. Fish caught in the brush weirs were dip-netted into boats at low or ebb tide or, if the water was low enough, loaded directly into carts. To remove the scales the men, in oiled

Smoke sheds at Woodward's Cove,
Grand Manan.

trousers and boots tied tightly around, scuffed
backward and forward among the fish without
lifting their feet from the "ceiling"—the bottom—of the boat. Today, the
scales are removed by machine and sent to a factory in Eastport for
manufacture into guanine or pearl essence, an iridiscent material that among
other uses adds gloss to lipstick and sheen to costume jewellery. In modern
weirs a weighted net (a purse-seine) is dropped vertically into the water and
the ends drawn in. The trapped fish are dip-netted in the traditional way or, if
the catch is heavy and the weir in deeper water, suction-pumped directly into
a sardine carrier.

But the problem for Quoddy region fishermen was not how to catch the fish, which were abundant, but how to market them. The product was eminently perishable and the markets distant. Herring, in particular, were so plentiful that a single tide could bring ten times as many fish into a brush weir as could be used—a thousand barrels when the owners of the weir could use only a hundred. Brush weirs were so tightly interwoven that the smallest herring, which were useless for smoking, could not pass through them, and as it was impossible to separate the larger herring from the small, waste was general. If, as frequently happened, more fish were taken than could be used, the surplus was left to rot on the beach or loaded into wagons and used as field manure. Captain Robb, who was one of the first to comment on the practice, also wondered if the destruction of young herring fry deprived cod and other fish of their natural food, driving them from the coast into deep water.

Until they could be frozen or refrigerated, fish destined for distant markets had to be salted and then pickled, dried, or smoked. Salt was a return cargo from Turks Island in the Bahamas but in Passamaquoddy's first fishing settlement, on Indian island, salt was made by boiling sea water in large kettles over a wood fire. Only a few large trees are left on Indian Island. When landed, ground fish were split, gutted, lightly salted, and wind dried on open wooden platforms or "flakes" until they were "as hard as chips." The fish were then barreled and marketed, the choice cod going to New York and Boston and the best pollock to the lumber camps. Fish of inferior quality usually ended up in the West Indies. Because of its poor salting properties relative to cod and pollock, the now-prized haddock was of little commercial importance.

Unlike ground fish, herring were usually smoked. After salting, the fish were threaded by their gills onto long sticks and then hung in crude smoke houses: tall buildings with rough board walls, a gabled roof with slats over the joints to keep out the rain, and an inside lining of mud or brick several feet high to prevent burning. Fish were usually dried and smoked wherever they were taken, so any patch of hospitable shore adjacent to a weir might have had flakes, storage sheds, a smoked herring stand, and seasonal quarters for families and workers.

Often the weirs were on islands, or the passages between islands, or between islands and the mainland, these being favourite herring runs. In Cow and Cheney passages, between Ross, Cheney and Whitehead islands off the south coast of Grand Manan, herring could strike in unimaginable numbers. Whitehead Island, in its late 19th century heyday, had five weirs and fifty smoked herring stands. During the season a hundred or more labourers would come from Maine and Nova Scotia to work "in the fish." Wood Island, also off Grand Manan and close to the heart of the herring schools, was another favoured fishing ground and during the season entire families moved there from Deep Cove and other places.

Yet despite the abundance of fish, there were few prosperous fishermen. Throughout the first half of the 19th century, observers expressed surprise at the poverty of the fishing communities. Moses Perley, who inspected the fishery in 1850, attributed it to inefficient methods of fishing and marketing and low standards of education. In response to Perley's report, the province sponsored fishery societies that, like agricultural societies, were expected to advance the industry. The Campobello Society established an annual fish fair at Welshpool that each autumn offered prizes for the best quality of fish. The fair, which became a society event, lasted until the beginning of this century.

An earlier, and in some ways more probing investigation than Perley's, had attributed the backwardness of the fishing industry to ignorance of Adam Smith's principle of the division of labour. The investigators, members of a government commission which sat on Grand Manan in 1836, concluded that an island "more happily situated for an extensive Fishery than any other spot on the coast of America" ought to have had men who did nothing but fish. Instead, deplored the commissioners, each man was a jack of all trades: a farmer, woodsman, and occasional carrier as well as a fisherman. While conceding that fishing and winter work in the woods might have complemented each other, the commissioners thought that farming and fishing, both summer occupations, were in fruitless competition.

But in addition to losing the advantages of specialization, island men also

Boat shed and loading platform, Stuart Town, Deer Island. In the days of a thriving inshore fishery, virtually every cove and inlet had facilities for storing boats and landing and drying fish.

lost the advantages of cooperation; a life of fishing and farming produced scattered settlement. Taking a leaf from developments in the highlands and islands of Scotland, where divided energies had also been perceived as a problem, the commissioners recommended that the government purchase sites for villages around the principal harbours, and that lots for a house and garden be granted on the understanding that the recipients work exclusively in the fishery.

No villages were planned and none, as events unfolded, were needed. In the second half of the century Grand Manan became a community of fishermen as singleminded as any of the 1836 commissioners could have wished. The catalysts were breakwaters, funded by the provincial government in the middle of the century, that converted exposed harbours into safe all-weather anchorages. When winds blew from the wrong quarter boats—of necessity small—had to be hauled ashore. Safe anchorages meant larger vessels and the possibility of tapping the deeper, richer waters offshore that hitherto only mainland fishermen from New England and Nova Scotia had been able to exploit. Handlining from small boats inshore continued but it became incidental to the offshore fishery.

The second half of the century also saw great activity in Grand Manan's smoked herring industry and the rise at Seal Cove of a close packed battery of smoke houses. As tasty thirst-makers, boneless smoked herring fillets captured the American bar trade, and their poorer cousins, unboned and unfilleted whole herring, the West Indian market. By 1875, Grand Manan was the world's largest producer of smoked herring and no longer a community of subsistent farmer/fishermen. There was also quantitative change: between 1860 and 1880 the population increased from 1,500 to 2,500. It is 3,500 today, and not a farmer amongst them.

Eastport, Lubec and the Sardine Industry ᴈ

The chief clearing houses for Passamaquoddy fish were Eastport and its neighbour Lubec. In return for granting Maine fishermen access to the provincial fishery, New Brunswick fishermen paid no duties when landing fish at Maine ports. When in Eastport or Lubec, they invariably picked up supplies. Trade was largely free on all the islands, and on Grand Manan absolutely so; with no customs officer on the island until 1867, Grand Mananers, as Moses Perley noted with evident envy, enjoyed "a perfect free trade."

Eastport and Lubec, both fishing ports in their own right, had every facility for handling unprocessed fish: smoke houses, fields for flaking or drying

on the edge of town, warehouses for storing salt, cranes for hoisting the fish and, in Moses Perley's phrase, "easy stairs" for the fishermen. In 1850, Eastport had about sixty wharves and a salt works on the southern edge of the island. The raw salt came from Turks Island in the Bahamas and Trapani in Italy and was processed at a rate of a thousand bushels a day.

Lobsters trapped during the season can now be held in pounds kept cool by tidal waters, fed a diet of herring, and marketed throughout the year. The road serving this Deer Island pound is, like several in the Quoddy region, submerged at flood tide. The first lobster pound was built on Deer Island (by Ed Conley) in 1928.

Though effective and cheap, curing with salt, wind and smoke could accommodate only ground fish and the larger herring. Small herring and shellfish, such as lobsters, scallops, and clams that throve in the sheltered bays, were impossible to get to market and therefore of no commercial value. At the beginning of settlement, lobsters were so plentiful that they could be picked up at low water or taken from a boat with a gaff—a cod hook with the barb removed—or even a forked stick. After storms had driven them onto the beaches in windrows, it was not uncommon for them to be hauled onto the fields as fertilizer.

In the absence of refrigeration and rapid transport, the answer to marketing perishable shellfish was to pack them in hermetically sealed containers. By 1850, plants at Eastport and nearby Treat's Island were canning salmon, lobster and codfish, and and by the mid-1860s there were small lobster canneries on Grand Manan and at St Andrews. An average Grand Manan lobster, so it was said, would fill four one-pound cans. The lobster shells, which made valuable top dressing, were spread over neighbouring fields.

But the great breakthrough in Eastport's canning industry came with the arrival of the sardine. In 1870 the Franco-Prussian war threatened New York's supply of French and Baltic, or "Russian," sardines, forcing importers to look for a supply of small herring that they could process and can. A case of imported French sardines that cost six to eight dollars in 1865, cost fifteen to twenty in 1870. Alerted by boxes of smoked Passamaquoddy herring in the New York markets, one of the importers, Julius Wolff, turned to the Eastport/Lubec area and began shipping small herring to New York where they were spiced and packed in handmade wooden kegs and sold as "Russian" sardines. To save shipping costs, and ensure a supply of fresh sardines, in 1875 Wolff's company (Wolff and Reessing) moved its operations to Eastport where it produced both "Russian" sardines and, copying French techniques, "fish in tin boxes." The first cannery was on lower Sea Street next to the wharf were the herring were landed. An advertisement calling for 5,000 barrels of small herring galvanized the moribund weir fishery. Everybody and his brother, as the Eastport historian Hugh French remarked, wanted part of the action.

By 1882 there were eighteen canneries in Eastport, four in Lubec and one in Robbinston. In 1886, the peak year of the industry, there were thirty-two plants on the American side of the Bay, not including can-making plants in Eastport and Lubec operating virtually year-round to build an inventory for the canning season. In Eastport, too, there was a mustard mill and a sawmill that made box material for packing the cans of sardines. Handy to the Eastport canneries was a wharf two hundred feet long by about a hundred wide piled high with barrels of cottonseed oil, which replaced expensive olive oil. Sardines were cooked in an oven and then placed in oil: "Fish biled in ile," as the local saying went.

The mid-1880s also saw the beginning of the New Brunswick sardine industry, slower to start than the one in Maine because of a prohibitive American tariff against imported sardines and, until the completion of a transcontinental railway system, no domestic market. But by 1885 there were small canneries at St Andrews and Black's Harbour, and by the early 1900s canneries on Deer Island, Campobello and Grand Manan.

The chief suppliers to the canneries were weir fishermen on Deer Island, Campobello and Grand Manan. Ninety-five percent of the herring canned in Eastport and Lubec came from the Canadian side. With sardine canning, the weir came into its own. Young herring feed near the shore and the weir was a natural method of impounding and, by enforced fasting, cleaning them. Fish caught by purse seiners out at sea are usually "feedy."

Herring were also taken in "shut-offs" or narrow-mouthed coves known to have herring in them. The mouth of the cove was shut off with twine netting and the cove seined in the same way as a weir. The sardine carriers, or "carry-away" boats, were sail driven at first but once gasoline engines became available sails were quickly replaced. Calm weather was the enemy of the canneries and to get the perishable herring into the wharves as quickly as possible sailboats frequently had to be hauled in tandem by steam-driven tugs.

The sardine industry revolutionized life on the islands. J.B. Mather's characterization of Campobello as "a Miserable reminant of poor fishermen" who paid rent in "produce, dried fish, or potatoes" and who occupied dilapidated buildings, was as true in 1875 as it had been in 1835. Conditions on Deer Island were no better. Before Deer Islanders built their weirs, noted the *Eastport Sentinel,* they had been living in old weather-beaten houses and fishing from leaky boats. Thanks to the sardine industry, they were able to fix their houses and now had "as nice a fleet of boats as any in the Bay. They owe it all," chimed the *Sentinel,* "to herring."

As well as catching the young herring, people from the islands also worked in the canneries. While the men tended the weirs and brought in the fish, women and children—some so small that they had to stand on boxes to reach the work tables—cut, cleaned, and packed fish. Herring were scooped out of the boats into storage tanks and then dumped from baskets onto the cutting tables, made slightly concave to keep the fish from falling off. The fish were then spread with a "spudger," a blunt, long-handled wooden rake, and despatched by darting hands and flashing knives. A practiced cutter, even with a fistful of fish, could remove head and entrails with a single stroke.

The canning season ran from mid-April to the end of November but until midsummer the herring runs were usually slow. For the cutters and packers, hours were

Built as a sail-driven sardine carrier in 1916, the now-motorized *Alma Connors* is still carrying herring. Here it is entering a weir off Grand Manan to load herring for the Connors Brothers plant at Black's Harbour on the New Brunswick mainland.

A yacht-built version of the "beamy" Lubec pinky sailing in Penobscot Bay, Maine. The original pinky was designed to hold large quantities of herring and to weather rough seas.

irregular, the workers being called when supplies of fish arrived at the factory wharf. Boys in Eastport, according to one droll visitor from Lewiston, played marbles with long, sharp "buccaneerish" knives tucked into in their belts. The signal to work was a single whistle for packers, two for flakers and three for sealers. Each company had a whistle of distinctive note, in one case a high pitched shriek that earned the offending plant the nickname the "Squealing Pig." At the sound of the whistles the cutters poured onto the streets, their foot-long, razor-sharp cutting knives either in hand or wrapped in the oil cloth capes that seasoned workers used to keep the "mush"—a rich mixture of oil, offal and fish flakes—off their clothing. The mush and the cuttings, called "pomee," were made into fertilizer.

In the 1880s there were seventeen canneries on Eastport's waterfront, each employing from forty to more than a hundred people. Usually they were two-storey frame buildings with a corrugated iron roof to minimize the damage should they catch fire. Hot oil and flame were uneasy partners and there were frequent conflagrations. The plants were named with the wry humour that is the only weapon of the unorganized and poorly paid: "Battleaxe," "Honey Pot," "Wrangle," "Starvation," "Penny Catcher," "Devil's Half Acre." The workers, who were mostly seasonal, lived or "bunged around" wherever they could find a roof and a bed: in cheap boarding houses, shanties, derelict buildings, storesheds, and even the crumbling barracks of old Fort Sullivan. The custodian of the Fort reported in 1891 that 150 squatters from the provinces had moved into the old barracks and—the fort's drains having given trouble from the day they were laid—that sewage flowed over the surface. Drunkenness, rowdyism, and street brawling were endemic in the town and at their worst in "Sodom," Eastport's once notorious south end that the lost entered, appropriately enough, via a bridge over a cove.

But like all brash manufacturing towns, Eastport then was vital. Warehouses and sardine canneries lined the shore and on fine Saturdays boats from Campobello, Deer Island and Grand Manan crowded into the harbour. Other revellers came by ferry from Lubec and Campobello. Sidewalks were thronged with strollers, shoppers, bootblacks and peanut vendors. Stores bursting with produce were open until ten or eleven P.M., barbers 'til even later. There were dances, band concerts, excursions to Calais, and on moonlit nights even musical evenings as a band played from a boat anchored in the Bay. When all movement was by water Eastport was mecca for the surrounding islands, and, on the larger map, doorway to a continent. While this centrality and sardine canning lasted, Eastport boomed.

THREE

MAKING A LANDSCAPE

PAUL VIDAL de la Blache, a revered
French geographer, once observed that a landscape is a
medal struck in the image of a people. By this he meant
that a society's ways, means, and values are expressed in
the pattern of roads, farms, villages and towns that it
imposes on the natural worlds. A glance or two at a

landscape can often tell us how a society sustains itself, while a closer look will reveal a good deal about values—what it considers important.

Though many of the Loyalists were moved less by political principle than by the commercial advantages of remaining within British North America, all in effect were refugees. By choosing to side with Britain and support the Crown, for whatever reasons, they had forfeited the comfort and security of a settled region for the privations of a wilderness. In their new place, it would have been inconceivable for their leaders not to have reaffirmed the principles that, at least in part, had led to their expulsion. To establish their superiority over the revolutionaries, whom they disdained as undisciplined and dangerous, the leaders determined to make New Brunswick the most orderly or, as one of them put it, "the most gentleman-like province on earth."

Decorous and orderly settlement called for a survey and a settlement plan. The first objective was to keep the troops from disbanded regiments in line by swift and rational settlement and the immediate imposition of civil authority. In New Brunswick, Colonel Edward Winslow remarked, there would be none of that "licentious behaviour that enforced idleness produces among soldiers." To ease the transition from military to civil authority, magistrates were chosen from the officer class. "It was our first proposal," wrote Winslow, "that the tract located for the provincials shou'd be formed in a County—that it shou'd be immediately organized—that magistrates shou'd be instantly appointed from among the officers so that before the men had loss'd their idea of military subordination they shou'd feel the more delicate restraint of civil authority." These arrangements, Winslow argued, would encourage the men to settle down and become "obedient and grateful subjects."

Thomas Carleton, governor of New Brunswick, hoped that the magistrates—who were appointed by the governor—would emulate the English justices of the peace. In 18th century England, justices were chosen almost exclusively from the landed gentry. Carleton's larger aim was a system of local government presided over by an officer class answerable to the governor and council, not the populace. The unit of local government was to be the parish,

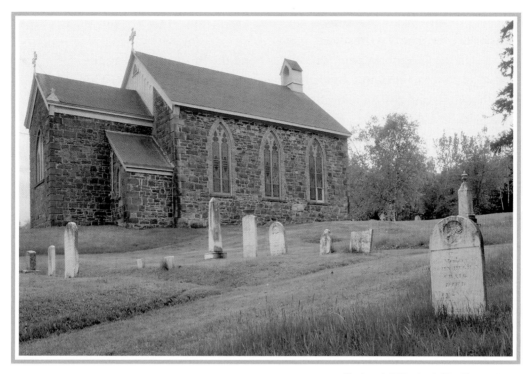

Shades of old England. The Chapel of Ease of St John the Baptist, Chamcook, built from local sandstone c. 1846.

with its old-world connotations of quietude and an unchanging social order, not the self-governing New England township.

The Carleton/Winslow prescription evidently worked. When the Reverend Jacob Bailey arrived in St Andrews in 1784 to report for the Society for the Propagation of the Gospel in Foreign Parts, he found that "the many bad, disorderly habits contracted during the war are declining apace, and the attention to order, religion and the education of children proportionably increases." According to Captain Peter Clinch of the Royal Fencible Americans, progress would have been even faster had the disbanded soldiers not had access to a virtual pipeline of West Indian rum. On the Magaguadavic he found that while provisions lasted, the soldiers "loiter[ed] around those places where rum was to be had, between which, and making a few shingles, catching fish, and hunting occasionally, the time was consumed."

On the St Andrews peninsula and around the shores of the Bay, the land, as in New England, was divided into farm or garden lots for distribution to both military and civilian refugees. The lots ran back from the shore in parcels of roughly one hundred acres and though not all were subsequently cleared and cultivated they provided for orderly and systematic agricultural settlement. Fields and pastures were laid out and the land broken and fenced. Almost forty percent of the men receiving town lots in St Andrews described themselves as farmer/yeomen and

Built in 1820 at the height of the town's prosperity, the Sheriff Andrews house, King Street, is a model of Georgian order and refinement. Elisha Andrews, sheriff of Charlotte County, was the son of the Reverend Samuel Andrews, the founding Anglican rector.

most of these eventually fanned out along the river and around the Bay.

In country districts, even well-to-do Loyalists had to do some roughing in the bush. In a frontier society where land was readily available, labour was virtually unobtainable. To Old World eyes, rural New Brunswick, as William Cobbett remarked, was a topsy turvey society of "Captains and colonels without soldiers" and "Squires without stockings and shoes." Loyalists with means who did manage to establish large estates invariably lost part of their investment. George Leonard cleared land in Sussex and built a house that, as Bishop Inglis recorded in his diary in 1792, resembled "a gentleman's villa in Europe." But by 1811, when Joseph Gubbins visited the now unkempt estate, its value had fallen from eight thousand pounds to three thousand.

Only settlers who arrived later, when labour was available, could ignore the frontier norms. One of these was Squire (John) Wilson, an Englishman who early in the 19th century settled with a number of his compatriots around Chamcook Bay, a few miles east of St Andrews. Wilson built saw mills and grist mills, cleared land for farming, and built a large brick house, Forest Lodge, in a beech wood that he attempted to stock with deer. His model was an English park in which sheep and deer graze peacefully around the house. In an effort to make an English village of the Chamcook settlement, Wilson and a neighbour promoted the building of an Anglican chapel by donating land and subscribing to a general fund. The Chapel of Ease of Saint John the Baptist is a corner of rural England on a foreign shore. There are neither yew trees nor stone walls, but the stone-built chapel, with its graveyard beside, lies beneath a wooded hill on a grassy knoll that overlooks the lovely Chamcook estuary.

St Andrews: A Planned Colonial Town ౨

FOR THE GENTLY SLOPING TOWNSITE, the Penobscot Loyalists adopted, like most settlers in new lands, a simple rectangular plan. Rectangular plans are the easiest to survey and, by providing lots of regular dimensions, the easiest to administer.

Chestnut Hall (1811), now the Ross Memorial Museum, takes up one corner of an intersection (King and Queen streets) considered by at least one historian of architecture to be the most attractive in Canada. In Chestnut Hall doors, windows, and even chimneys combine to convey a sense of balance and order.

But the St Andrews plan, though a grid-iron of straight streets and rectangular blocks, was not the unrelieved surveyor's plat that subsequently overtook towns and cities in the interior of the continent.

For surveyors in the colonies, the London-based Board of Trade and Plantations provided written guidelines for town layout. The ideal was a plan, or plat, about a mile square with a southerly orientation. In the centre of the plat or, in the case of coastal towns, in the centre of the waterfront, there was to be a public square or parade and four subsidiary squares equidistant from the centre. The squares were settings for market places, schools, hospitals and other community uses. Colonial surveyors were also required to reserve space for fortifications and barracks and, ominously for St

The rectory of All Saints, built c. 1790 and subsequently gifted to the church. The church is in the background, surrounded by greensward.

Andrews, forest land for the production of masts and spars for the Royal Navy.

Though rectangular plans were suited to the limited means of colonial and military surveyors, they were also the fashionable plans of 17th and 18th century Europe. Champlain's plan for the tiny settlement on St Croix Island was, as we have seen, a little grid. Rectangular planning, which originated in classical Greece and Rome and had been revived in Renaissance Italy, spread northward to France and England. By the 17th century, Parisian suburbs were being organized around formal squares, and after the Great Fire of 1666 several of the plans for the rebuilding of London were rectangular. None of the plans was adopted but one of them, by Richard Newcourt, might well have been the model for the Board of Trade's guidelines to colonial surveyors. From England formal, classical plans crossed the Atlantic, first to the American colonies, then to Canada. William Penn's plan for Philadelphia, for example, resembles Newcourt's plan for London.

The authors of the plan for St Andrews were faithful to their London masters. The orientation was southerly and the six streets paralleling the shore were approximately a mile long. The plan set aside two adjacent blocks in the centre of the waterfront for a market square, a church and public buildings, and four other blocks elsewhere in the plat for unassigned public uses. To prevent crowding and the spread of fires, the residential lots were generous (80ft. by 160ft.) and the streets ample. As in Philadelphia, the main street—running at a right angle to the waterfront—was to be wider than the rest (80ft. as opposed to 60ft.). The only departures from absolute symmetry were the uneven waterfront lots, the shore not being a straight line.

Although there was nothing in its plan to suggest that St Andrews was different in kind from the towns of the American

Although built of stone, not wood, Parson Andrews' cottage on Minister's Island, built c. 1790, was the archetypal folk house of the region. The shed is an addition.

seaboard, the street names told a different story. The front street nearest the shore, as is the custom in coastal towns, was named Water Street, but all the remaining streets had Royal associations. King, Queen, Princess Royal and Prince of Wales require no explanation. Others were named after Sir Guy Carleton, the commander in chief of the King's forces in North America, Colonel John Parr, governor of Nova Scotia, and thirteen of the royal children: Ernest, Adolphus, Montague, Augustus, Harriet, Elizabeth, etc.

But the royal aura, though particularly intense in St Andrews, covered the entire region. When the Loyalists on the north side of the Bay of Fundy hived off to form a province separate from Nova Scotia, they named the province after the House of Brunswick, to honour the King. The capital they named Fredericton after Frederic, the Duke of York and second son of George III; the county, of which St Andrews became the shiretown, they named Charlotte, after the Queen.

The houses and public buildings of the town complemented the symmetry of the streets. Georgian planning and building was all of a piece. A few of the buildings were Castine originals which had been taken apart and the pieces, in numbered lots, shipped to St Andrews for re-assembly. Among them was a coffee house and tavern (destroyed by fire in 1930) that in forthright 18th century fashion was re-assembled on the waterfront just below Water Street. But most buildings, however, were newly made from lumber and other materials provided by Great Britain.

In time, the merchant and professional families, often with the aid of pattern books, built substantial two-storey town houses in the Georgian or English Renaissance style then fashionable on the eastern seaboard. Its hallmarks were compact, rectangular shapes and balanced facades: a central doorway, usually with transom and sidelights in the grander houses, and well-proportioned windows arranged symmetrically on each side of the door. Exterior walls were generally of clapboard, but occasionally of brick, which was more expensive. Interiors were just as regular as exteriors, each floor having a pair of rooms—of roughly equal size—on each side of the central hallway and staircase. Order, order, everywhere.

One of the most elegant houses in the town was built in 1811 by Harris Hatch, a member of Her Majesty's council, commissioner of bankruptcies, registrar of deeds, and a lieutenant colonel in the Charlotte County militia. Although St Andrews was in a defensible border zone, the militia here, as elsewhere in the province, was more social and ceremonial than functional. Its officers were the leading figures in their communities and, as a rule, were either veterans of the Revolutionary War or the sons of veterans. Harris Hatch's house was built in the American Federal style with chimneys symmetrically arranged on each of the four corners, a hipped roof and the usual balanced facade. He called the house Chestnut Hall. Its principal rooms were decorated with elaborate plaster work and are said to have been the scene of lavish entertainments crowned by sumptuous meals provided by Violet, Colonel Hatch's black cook.

Well-proportioned Georgian houses laid out along straight, generous streets satisfied the Loyalist need for refinement and, though both street plan and house styles had been transmitted via New England and the middle colonies, they maintained links with an older and, in Loyalist eyes, more disciplined world. The symmetry and solidity of the houses, combined with the regularity of the streets, also suggested a measure of human control in what was, in effect, a raw wilderness. In nature there are no straight lines. A solid Georgian house standing four square to the elements was a perennial favourite in colonial paintings and embroideries. The houses of the ordinary folk in St Andrews, though simpler, were just as regular. Most were of the Cape Cod type.

Like the formal Georgian houses, the "Capes"—descendants of 17th century East Anglian cottages—were also of English provenance. Most were approximately square with a central chimney and stairway. The second storey nestled beneath a steeply pitched gabled roof. Parlours, kitchen and bedrooms were arranged neatly on each side of the chimney and stairway. Exteriors simply heralded the order within. Doorways were central in the facade and windows were well-proportioned and evenly spaced. Trim, if any, was restrained and economical; doorways were unadorned except for transom lights, and eaves and

gable ends were plain. Shingles, rather than clapboard, were the usual covering for both walls and roof. Low walls and tight eaves

Salt box houses, common in New England, are scarce in New Brunswick. This one was built c. 1785 by Joseph Crookshank, a ship's carpenter.

made for ease and efficiency in heating while the massive chimney and large roof gave the house a snug, sheltering look. These were critical attributes in a climate the Loyalists found "inhospitable."

Institutional buildings were also models of restraint and, in a few cases, elegance. The town's first church, Anglican by decree, was a plain structure that served all denominations. It was built between 1788 and 1790, as a matter of conscious imperial policy, both British and colonial governments anticipating that the Church of England would become the people's church. It did not, but as the state church it served as an instrument of Loyalism. Indoctrination in its forms and order—the argument ran—would encourage loyalty to the Crown and, ipso facto, habits of obedience and acceptance. The implication being, of course, civil disorder in the American colonies might have been contained had more of the colonists held correct religious principles. In the eyes of the Loyalist leaders, however, membership in the Church of England and loyalty to Great Britain were one and the same. Other denominations were tolerated but they had no inherent rights within the body politic.

In St Andrews, as in the province as a whole, Presbyterians and Congregationalists outnumbered Anglicans but so great were the rewards of obeisance that dissent was expediently stifled. Sensing the compliant mood, the commissary of the London-based and government supported Society for the Propagation of the Gospel in Foreign Parts (SPG) recommended the appointment of a rector. Almost immediately the blessings of the establishment fell on the town. Most of the rector's salary as well as eighty percent of the costs of a new church building (the Church of St Andrews) were borne by the SPG and the New Brunswick government. So, too, were the costs of maintaining church-supported schools. For additional funds, the parish could draw on the income in rents and stumpage fees from glebe, or prime Crown lands, granted to it by the province. "Dissenting" churches received neither money nor land.

The first rector, the Reverend Samuel Andrews from Connecticut, was both a missionary of the SPG and, like most of the Episcopal clergy, an ardent royalist who openly espoused the English side. During the Stamp Act crisis of 1765 he delivered a sermon on the "duty of Obedience to the higher Powers," and at the time of the equally critical Continental Congress of 1775 he deplored the resistance to authority and appealed to his countrymen to do nothing "but what the laws of God approve." But whereas Samuel Andrews, a latitudinarian in doctrine, was able to mollify the nonconformist elements in his St Andrews congregation, his successor, J.M.H. Mercer, merely inflamed them. By stubbornly insisting that authority in all church matters rested with the clergy, a view that officially was shared by the SPG and the New Brunswick heads of the Church, he alienated the Presbyterians who began to leave shortly after his appointment in 1818.

Whatever the ecclesiastical consequences of the move, the architectural ones were a blessing. Modelled after Congregational churches in New England,

Greenock Presbyterian Church, completed in 1824, is a beautifully proportioned Wren-style church with the usual classical accoutrements: a pedimented doorway, palladian windows, and an octagonal belfry and spire. Interior columns supporting the galleries were made from local bird's eye maple and the imposing nail-free pulpit with mahogany from Honduras. The most striking embellishment, however, is the stylized green oak tree, carved on the base of the spire. Captain Christopher Scott, a successful mariner and merchant who financed the final stages of building, wanted a reminder of his birthplace: Greenock in Scotland.

Though more earthbound than the heavenward straining Greenock, the reigning Anglican Church is also a graceful building prominently located, like its predecessor, at the lower end of King Street. It was designed, in 1865, in the then popular perpendicular style by a Boston-based English church architect. Identifying characteristics of the style are vertical lines, a steeply pitched roof, wide bargeboards and pointed, Gothic windows. The original plans called for a stone building but costs were prohibitive and the vestry settled for New Brunswick spruce and pine, painted and, in places, plastered to look like stone. The church (All Saints) is set in glorious greensward that runs unbroken to its handsome rectory, a Georgian house gifted subsequently to the church.

Inside All Saints hang British and New Brunswick flags and inscribed in the central window of the sanctuary is the unequivocal motto: Fear God and Honour the King. But the most potent symbol of allegiance hangs in the west portal: a wood carving of the coat of arms of William and Mary (1688-1694) presented to the church at Wallingford in the once-loyal province of Connecticut and brought to St Andrews by the Reverend Samuel Andrews in 1786 or 1787. Royal coats of arms, marking the monarch's position as head of the Church of England, were standard appendages of English churches after the Restoration.

Equally symbolic of the town's allegiance is the magnificent County Courthouse, built in 1840 on an open square in the plat. Cast in the form of an Athenian temple with gable roof, pediment and doric columns, it stands on a crest—probably an ancient shoreline—just above the general level of the town.

The east window
of All Saints,
dedicated to the
Reverend
Samuel Andrews,
its first rector,
beseeches the
faithful to fear
God and honour
the King.

All Saints, St Andrews' immaculate Anglican Church. The original
design called for a stone building with a spire, but New Brunswick
pine and a square, Norman tower were more than adequate
substitutes.

St Andrews most visible symbol of Loyalism is the exquisite Charlotte County Courthouse built in 1840. The pediment, supported by Doric columns, frames the royal coat of arms with its uncompromising motto: *Dieu et Mon Droit.* To the right is the wall of the old gaol, now the home of the Charlotte County Archives.

"The building," noted the St Andrews *Standard,* "is situated on a rising ground ... and from its commanding situation it will have an imposing effect when completed." In a culture where height has virtue, justice should properly be dispensed from an elevation. The original courthouse had been built on low ground, above the gaol, in the business section of the town. Like most institutional buildings in thriving seaports it found itself crowded out of the waterfront.

Thomas Berry, the confident builder of the new courthouse, thought that justice should also be dispensed from a building with style and substance. To emphasize the classical form and structural solidity of the building, Berry added heavy pilasters of seasoned pine on each of the four exterior corners and on each side of the substantial double entrance door. By going beyond the requirements of the contract, Berry exceeded his budget by several hundred pounds but justified the expense on the grounds that without the embellishments the building would have looked "naked." With them, on the other hand, it was "superior to any public building of the kind in the province."

Classical revival styles were also popular in the United States but no American pediment frames a hand carved, brightly painted royal coat of arms with the uncompromising motto *Dieu et Mon Droit*. And in no American courthouse, too, will you find portraits of the reigning Queen, her great-great-grandmother Queen Victoria, and commissioned photographic reproductions of portraits of George III, his wife, Queen Charlotte, and

Water Street, St Andrews, on Canada Day.

thirteen of their fifteen children. The Gainsborough originals hang in the Queen's Gallery at Windsor Castle. The business section of the town, along the waterfront, was the usual mixture of shops, offices, storage sheds, and wharves, all vying— when trade flourished—for limited commercial space. In the few blocks on each side of the market square vessels were loaded and unloaded and goods and materials stored. Here, too, were the shops of merchants and craftsmen. Commercial building was substantial from the outset so there was no need, as in later frontier towns, for facades or false fronts to disguise shoddy construction or mean looking eaves. Some buildings, too, were built with their gable ends facing the street, so that a few blocks of Water Street would not look out of place in the older sections of Bristol or Bergen. The chandler, the tanner, the tinsmith, and the watchmaker have gone but the buildings remain, adapted, as in all historic streets, to new uses.

THE ISLANDS ↔

LOYALISTS WERE ALSO PROMINENT IN MOST of the island populations, but there were relatively few of them and only in Grand Manan were they first on the scene. There were no surveys to ensure neat and orderly settlement, and on Campobello and Deer Island the settlers had to contend with archaic systems of landholding and intransigent landlords. Distinctly Loyalist or British marks on the landscape are scarce. An occasional household may fly the Red Ensign (the old Canadian flag) or even a Union Jack but except for Anglican churches in Campobello and Grand Manan nothing in the design of the buildings or their layout suggests any particular provenance.

St Paul's in Grand Harbour, Grand Manan, was built ostensibly to dispel the "appalling religious ignorance" that Dr Jerome Alley of St Andrews had found there on a pastoral visit in 1820. But as in St Andrews, the decision to build an Anglican Church had political as well as religious implications. A building of the

Wesleyan and Baptist churches at Seal Cove, Grand Manan.

established church in the very centre of the inhabited west coast would not only be a reminder of British sovereignty (recently ratified in the agreement of 1817) but it might also stem the radical tide of Baptism that was then beginning to rise in all the islands. To apprehensive Anglicans in St Andrews and Fredericton, the islands and back country were beyond the religious pale: "outstations [of ignorant people]" according to Bishop Charles Inglis, "who easily succumb to the novel doctrines of the wild sectaries." A "wild sectary," in orthodox Anglican eyes, was a decentralized church that insisted on the authority of the Bible and advocated power to the laity and the locality. Baptism was the child of New England Congregationalism.

Such was the egalitarian temper of early 19th century Grand Manan that even in the new Anglican church the altar, following the New England Congregationalist tradition, was set in the middle of the congregation. In English

St Anne's Church, Campobello.

churches the altar was always at the east end of the nave, distancing the clergy from their flocks. The independence of the laity unsettled the first minister, an intemperate young Englishman (Cornelius Griffin) sent to the island in 1824 by the SPG: "Each one," he noted, "thinks himself as much a king as the King of England." Careless, too, about regular times of worship they were clearly "too proud to be taught their Duty to GOD and man."

Almost from its inception, St Paul's was riven with a feud that led, in 1839, to the burning in effigy of the Reverend John Dunn, the first rector, the deliberate firing of the building, a criminal trial in St Andrews at which sixty island men testified, and the defection to the Baptists of one of the protagonists. The new church, built largely with funds solicited in Britain, was made of stone.

Even more of a rearguard action was St Anne's in Campobello, built by Admiral Fitz-William Owen in 1855. Promoted by the evangelical movement, the New Light, founded by the Nova Scotian Henry Alline, Baptism was sweeping the

Houses and a boat shed backing onto the shore at Wilson's Beach, Campobello.

island. Its ideals of power to the laity, rather than the clergy, and of taking the Bible as sole authority in matters of faith and practice, appealed not only to the Americans at Wilson's Beach but also to many of the descendants of the original Loyalists. Sensing perhaps that a new church building, replacing the "rude" structure built by David Owen, would not prevent defection, the pragmatic Admiral Fitz-William Owen offered a gift to mammon: three years of free pasture lands to all households within the Anglican fold.

Whereas St Andrews was planned and built at a stroke, the island settlements grew slowly and organically. There were no surveys and settlement

Plain Cape Cod cottages were once standard housing on the islands. This one is a replica, built at Whale Cove, Grand Manan, for the novelist Willa Cather.

plans. People gathered loosely around sheltered coves and bays and built in ways that custom and function directed. Access to the sea was the first priority. People built simple houses in places where fish could easily be landed and washed, and where there was space for the construction of fish stages, flakes, and smokehouses. Land for gardens, pasture and field crops was taken in from the woods and the waste as it was needed. Because stages, flakes and fields took up large amounts of space a small number of families could fill a cove. Once a cove was filled, new arrivals moved on to the next.

Surveys conducted after the settlement merely registered existing improvements. With no zoning regulations or town or village councils to direct growth, people lived where they liked. Although choices were guided by convenience and use, the effect could seem aimlessly picturesque. As two American visitors wrote affectingly of one Deer Island settlement in 1908: "Its houses seem to have gone wandering aimlessly along the shore on one forgotten day, and to have paused suddenly in their tracks, never, for some unapparent reason, to move again." Occasionally, the houses stopped in such a way that there are front and "back" roads, the front road paralleling the shore with the "back," and sometimes less reputable, road some distance behind.

In the fishing settlements most people chose to be neighbourly, living close by family and friends. For a newly married son or daughter, a meadow might be converted into a building lot and a new path made to connect it to the existing family home. Proximity and daily contacts were far more important than privacy or quiet. Yards in fishing communities, as the Newfoundland folklorist Gerald Poucis pointed out, tend to be friendly, welcoming spaces, often filled with ornaments, not formal moats protecting the houses.

EASTPORT ᴣ

ON THE ISLANDS AND ALONG THE SHORE, conditions of settlement were similar on both sides of the line. In Maine, most of the townships in the state were granted to individuals, companies or institutions. Township number 8, now Eastport and Lubec, had never been granted or surveyed so that for the first ten or twelve years the settlers were squatters. In an attempt to accommodate the improvements of each settler, a survey conducted in 1791 subdivided Moose Island into twenty-four 100-acre lots. But most of the lots, which could only approximate the improvements, were quickly broken up so that by 1834 only one of the originals remained.

As on the British islands, the first settlers built wherever they could conveniently conduct their business, making do initially with a makeshift log house for living quarters, and a shed or smoke house for curing fish. The town had to wait ten or twelve years for its first framed building. Because there was no plan, all the shore land was eventually taken up, leaving no room for parks or public spaces. With no SPG or government support of any kind, churches and schools were slow to appear, and in the town's rambunctious early days there seems to have been little enthusiasm for either. At the time of the British capture in 1814, there was no settled minister in the town and no established church building. The only preacher in the place, according to the arch *Essex Register,* was "a smooth tongued man accounted one of the sleekest smugglers there." At a town meeting in 1800, Eastporters voted down a tax to sustain a resident minister.

Education fared no better. One of the first schools occupied one half of a small house on Water Street; the other half was a tavern. The owner, Mr Greenwood, functioned as both teacher and barman. Legend has it that while he attended to daytime topers, his pupils performed eight-handed reels to a chorus sung by the occupants of both rooms. The frolics at Mr Greenwood's short-lived school (1793-1794) clearly lost nothing in the telling but records of town meetings between 1798 and 1810 suggest that schooling was hardly a priority. In two of the twelve years (1798 and 1803) schools were voted no taxes at all, and in the remaining years amounts varied from $100 to $175. Between 1800 and 1810 the town's population rose from 500 to 1500.

In Eastport, as in all the coastal communities, virtually all movement was by water and all that mattered was access to it; people used boats in the same way as city people used carriages, and they undertook long voyages as a matter of course. The town had wharves long before it had streets or roads. Warehouses, stores, and business offices were built around them. Houses, churches, and schools were all back of the waterfront. The first road in Eastport was laid out in 1799, nearly twenty years after the first settlement. Describing it was a nightmare for the selectmen: "Beginning at Mr James Cochran's spring, between Captain Prince's house and the house Mr Henry Waid now lives in, and running northerly between said Cochran's house and his old hovel, and just to the westward of Mr Samuel Tuttle's barn, through the corner of his potato field, to the west corner of Mr Shackford's field ... through Mr Boynton's and Mr Henry Poor's land to the notch in

Eastport Harbour with downtown.

Mr William Clark's mountain ... to the upper end of
the island." Because there was virtually no wheeled traffic, gates and bars obstructed
town roads until 1808.

Between Eastport and other communities the only land connections were
footpaths through the woods or, if the woods had been cleared, the stumps. No
one ever considered walking if there was a boat available. There was no road to
Dennysville until 1806 and none to Robbinston until 1809-1810. In a letter to a
friend in 1811, an itinerant missionary travelling by horse wrote that "the road
from Robbinston to Dennysville is worse than I ever saw or you ever heard
before." Rocks, roots, mud and mire were so deep that the horse "could scarcely
get along." Jonathan Weston, Eastport's first historian, was the first Moose

Islander to cover the entire distance to Machias by land, in 1806. He recalled the excitement and even fear caused by a horse being brought onto the island in 1804. Samuel Jones of Robbinston swam his horse across the channel from Pleasant Point to Carlow's Island and rode along the bars and beaches and through the woods to the town. Children rushed to see the strange animal and one is said to have remarked: "There goes a man sitting on a cow that ain't got any horns."

Horses, wagons and carriages were just as scarce elsewhere. Though on the mainland, St Andrews was really accessible only by water. The river road to St Stephen was extremely difficult and the road to Saint John a roller coaster ride across ridges and through cedar swamps. In 1851 a visiting English agronomist, J.F.W. Johnston, described it as "long and rough." Deer Island is said to have been without horses until the middle of the century, and mounted or wheeled traffic was so unusual that paths and roads, as in Eastport, were an obstacle course of bars and gateways. In the 1870s there were forty pairs of bars on the narrow road between Cummings Cove and Fairhaven, a distance of about two miles.

Because all the settlements looked seaward, all developed in partial isolation. Markets were seldom, if ever, local and only zealous missionaries and determined agronomists travelled overland. As a result, communities developed independently of each other, each with its own school and churches. There was not much intermingling. Thus developed a range of local accents, usually only minor variations on a basic theme, but to the experienced ear often identifiable. All, of course, signalled the world from which the original inhabitants came. Seal Covers may now have suppressed all republican sentiments, but as long as a horseless carriage is a "cah," officials in Fredericton and Ottawa may still wonder if the fellows are good Canadians.

THE LANDSCAPE OF LEISURE

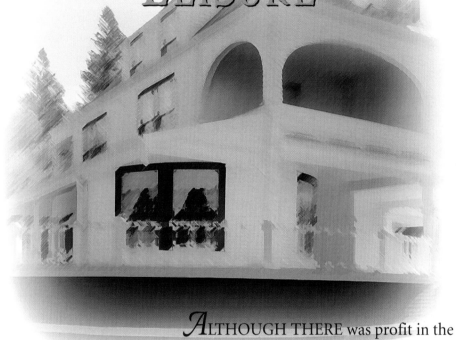

$\mathcal{A}$LTHOUGH THERE was profit in the lumber and carrying trades, the prosperity it brought was fragile. The demand for Maritime lumber and shipping depended on the preferential treatment given to colonial goods in British markets and on Great Britain's prosecution of her restrictive navigation laws. Patrick Campbell, that astute Scottish observer, had seen the danger of protectionism as early as 1794: "This settlement," he wrote of St Andrews, "is at present in a prosperous state; but it is feared it will not continue long so, on account of the American States being able to export their lumber to Britain on as low a duty as those of our Colonies; and as their country is full of people, and labour cheap, they can undersell us in our own markets." Without a trade in lumber, he concluded direly, "this town or county cannot subsist."

The first blow fell in 1830 when Britain announced its intention of opening West Indian markets to American shipping. Even the prospect of cheaper American goods was enough to leave laden Maritime vessels stranded in tropical harbours. In 1831 Captain George McAllister, master of the St Stephen brig *Keziah,* was unable to sell a cargo of boards and shingles in Carlisle Bay, Barbados, even though lumber was scarce on the island: "The people," McAllister wrote in his journal, "run of an idea that they will get Boards for nothing almost of the Americans as well as every other thing and I cannot say but this expectation may be realized in a measure as they [the Americans] are crowding in for the first market." McAllister sailed on to Tobago, where he failed again, and finally to Trinidad where he managed to find buyers.

For the St Croix and Passamaquoddy ports the repeal of the navigation laws and the dropping of the colonial preference were hammer blows from which they never recovered. The value of St Andrews' exports to the West Indies fell from 104,000 pounds in 1829 (roughly two thirds of its total annual exports) to 36,000 pounds in 1834. Indian Island and Campobello, both major entrepôts for West Indian goods, were also devastated. Indian Island, especially, lived by the West Indian trade. Rum, sugar and molasses, brought back as return cargoes from the West Indies, were re-shipped from the islands to ports in New England and elsewhere in the Maritimes. In 1827 Indian Islanders owned thirteen vessels; in 1835 only one.

At the same time as Yankee traders were "crowding in" on West Indian markets, lumber exports to Britain were falling off. The British market remained protected until 1842 but by this time lumbering on the St Croix had moved well upstream. There were still marketable trees around St Andrews but most were in blocks reserved for the Royal Navy. Within the reserves all pines considered suitable for masts became the King's property and were marked with his broad arrow. The two largest naval holdings lay immediately behind the farm lots of St Andrews.

Shipbuilding also suffered as the lumber trade dwindled and colonial markets, no longer protected, began to recede. The decline was slow at first but became headlong when steam and iron began to replace wood and sail. By 1860 the sound of hammers and caulking malls had virtually died along the river and out in the islands. In 1857 the only hammer to be heard in any of the yards between Calais and Eastport, according to the *Eastport Sentinel,* was the auctioneer's. Boats were still built for the fishery and the coastal trade but the demand from these could hardly sustain a major industry.

For want of alternatives, people went back to the land and the middle years of the century saw a brief flowering of agriculture. Between 1840 and 1851 the amount of improved land in Charlotte County almost doubled, to reach record levels. Along the St Croix immediately above St Andrews, in the district of Bayside, farmers had found a cash crop: turnips. When the only vegetables available were northern and seasonal, the hardy and tasty turnip was a popular domestic dish. The turnip grows well in cool climates and when, as in Bayside, the drills were fertilized with a compost of mussel mud, rotten fish, rockweed and barnyard manure, good crops were virtually guaranteed. The most potent elixir, as reported to visiting agronomist J.F.W. Johnston, was mussel-mud applied while the mussels were still alive. Eventually, through a deficiency of boron (a mineral nutrient) in the soil, the turnips developed black hearts but when healthy they brought good prices in the Boston market. "See Boston or die a fool" was the watchword of late 19th century Bayside: the barreled turnips were shipped south in schooners.

In an effort to revive Campobello's flagging economy, Admiral Fitz-William Owen and a handful of associates from St Andrews and elsewhere floated, in 1839, the Campobello Mill and Manufacturing Co. The aim was to convert the island's fish, trees and wool into marketable commodities by building tide-generated mills to saw lumber and full cloth. Capital was to be invested in fishing and farming and there were even plans for a new town near the head of

Old turnip fields in Bayside, a few miles above St Andrews. In the background is Dochet's Island, lost against the woods of Maine. Until recently the house in the foreground was a summer residence of John Turner, the former prime minister of Canada.

the narrows opposite Lubec. Like the commissioners who examined the Grand Manan fishery, in 1836, the principals frowned on fishing/farming combinations.

On Campobello fishing, not farming, was the culprit: "from the indolent habits they acquire as fishermen," noted Admiral Owen, "they pay but little attention to their farms." A few sawmills were built and a few machines for carding wool may have been imported but despite printing a prospectus and offering two thousand shares at $200 each the company never materialized.

After 1850 populations began to decline as the native-born moved away and immigration from Europe came to an end. Only Grand Manan, whose fisheries expanded in the second half of the century, managed to stem the tide. Eastport, no longer a smuggling citadel and with its fisheries in decline and the coasting trade almost gone, suffered small but steady population losses (from 4,125 to 3,736) between 1850 and 1870. It also lost property when, in 1864, a fire driven by winds off the harbour destroyed the business district and many of the wharves and warehouses. It recovered dramatically with the arrival of sardine canning in the 1870s, but as the sardine industry declined so did its population. From a peak of 5,300 at the turn of the century it has now fallen to fewer than 2,000.

In Eastport and Lubec, sardine canning fell before a combination of blows; chief among them were a sharp decline in US consumption after World War I, destructive price cutting by the canneries, and the whittling away of protective tariffs against foreign competition. By contrast, the Canadian industry, controlled by the Connors brothers in Black's Harbour, had far more staying power. There was no destructive price cutting, and by consolidating their operations in Black's Harbour and integrating them vertically they reduced costs and safeguarded supplies of both materials and labour. Connors Brothers made their own cans and crates and provided housing for their workers. And with outlets in the Caribbean, Europe, Africa and Mexico as well as Canada, they were not dependent on the American market.

Campobello and Deer Island also stagnated. In a final flourish of landlordism, Captain Robinson-Owen, Campobello's last principal proprietary, insisted that rents during the Civil War (1861-1865) be paid in coin from Britain, not inflated American bills. Tenants unable to pay are said to have lost all or part of their properties, one of the victims being an infirm old man with a debt of $23.00. Both islands benefited from the sardine industry, their populations holding their own or even increasing a little, but since 1891 Deer Island's population has declined by half, to just over 800.

With no carrying trade to sustain it, Indian Island's population dwindled away—finally, to nothing. A few of the houses became summer homes but the rest, like the wharves and the storage sheds, fell to wind and weather. St Andrews, too, seemed doomed. The loss of the British and West Indian trade was a disastrous blow. From being an important link in the commerce of the Atlantic, St Andrews suddenly found itself on the remote edge of a continent that no

Campobello. The Wells-Shober Cottage, one of five cottages that are now part of the Roosevelt Campobello International Park.

longer looked to Europe and the West Indies. With its shipping and lumber trade gone, the town was on its last legs. It managed to stay neat and trim but as early as 1836 its trade, as the historian Peter Fisher noted, "appear[ed] to be dwindling away without any satisfactory prospect of revival."

To stop the rot, a group of businessmen—among them Squire John Wilson of Chamcook—struck on a vaulting idea: to make St Andrews the winter port of Canada by building a trunk line to the interior. St Andrews was closer to Montreal than any other Maritime port and, like all the Atlantic ports, it was ice-free. In 1835 there were no railways in Canada and the first American railroad was only five years old.

In thrall to rail and steam, the British Government advanced 10,000 pounds for a survey, and Squire Wilson brought in a boatload of Irish navvies, but when word reached Washington that the intention was to run the line through territory then in dispute between Maine and New Brunswick the scheme had to be shelved. For St Andrews, whose chief hope lay in seizing the moment and wresting the prize from stronger rivals, the delay was critical. By 1842, the year of the Webster/Ashburton Treaty which settled the boundary dispute, Saint John and Halifax had both decided that they, too, would make excellent Atlantic termini.

Yet construction of a line to Quebec did begin and though never completed it brought Aroostook potatoes and a little extra lumber to St Andrews. But the revival was the last flicker in the tail of a dying economy. In 1860, a visitor returning after a twelve year interval found the town to be "dull, dilapidated, and in need of paint." Idle men, looking like "shipwrecked sailors on a deserted isle," sauntered dejectedly about the streets and wharves, and a shore that once was alive with sail became a catchpit for unwanted schooners and barges. As the town's economy collapsed people drifted away. The population halved between 1850 and 1880 and by the beginning of this century it had fallen to fewer than 2,000, roughly its current size. St Andrews had become, as a disconsolate resident described it in 1878, "a Sunday town." With no rail connection to the interior, and no hope for a revival of its Atlantic trade, St Andrews was down and virtually out.

THE TOURIST TRADE ॐ

YET THE TOWN SURVIVED. The Penobscot Loyalists had chosen better than they knew. A peninsular location with no appreciable hinterland may have been vulnerable to shifts in the currents of trade but it enabled the town to profit from one of the growth industries of the second half of the 19th century: tourism.

Blessed with scenery and, as its early promoters put it, a "salubrious and healthful climate," St Andrews had two priceless assets. The St Croix River and Passamaquoddy Bay would grace any scenic canon and Fundy air, cooled by the huge tidal exchanges that in summer kept sea water around a frigid 10°C (50°F), was a salve to people seeking relief from continental heat.

Even Patrick Campbell, who saw everything in terms of utility, had felt bound to note that St Andrews was "prettily situated." Much more effusive was Edward Winslow, the prominent Loyalist. During a visit in 1810, he declared the town and its setting to be "by far the most interesting and most delightful part of the province of New Brunswick." Winslow was recovering from an attack of gout and relief may have coloured his judgement, but later in the century other prominent Maritimers, in whom there was no suspicion of post-gout euphoria, were of the same mind. Sir Leonard Tilley, leader of New Brunswick's reluctant march to Confederation, and prospective lieutenant governor of the province, became a summer resident in 1871. A jealous Saint John editor accused him of "burrowing" in some town along the border, but within a year Sir Charles Tupper had followed Sir Leonard's example. Sir Charles was also a "Father of Confederation" and for a season, in 1896, he was prime minister.

By 1881, local entrepreneurs had built two summer hotels: the Argyle, near the point on the peninsula, and Kennedy's—today's Shiretown Inn—on Water Street. The populace, too, turned entrepreneur by assessing itself $10,000 at a ratepayers meeting to float a hotel company. St Andrews, according to the editor of one of the town's two newspapers, was well on its way to becoming the "Saratoga of the East." But enthusiasm and local enterprise do not make national or international resorts, as the editor knew well. Major developments would require, as he put it, "new blood" and "new men."

Inevitably, these came from the great cities of the east. Railways and steamships by this time had opened up the hinterlands of New York, Boston and Montreal and awakened the urban rich to the therapeutic and recreational possibilities of what had been, until then, inaccessible back country. Any attractive coastal or lakeside town that could provide relief from heat and

The "great Bay of Passamaquoddy." The vessels in the harbour are nearly all pleasure boats and the weir is an attractive relic. In the foreground is one of the most picturesque holes in the entire gallery of golf; in the misty distance, Deer Island.

humidity, and was within a day's travel of a metropolis, was a potential summer resort. The keys to success were a cool climate and picturesque surroundings.

For most of the 19th century there was no medicine as we know it. Until Pasteur demonstrated, in 1864, that diseases were transmitted by invisible organisms with antecedents, there was no certain knowledge of the causes of infection. So radical was Pasteur's hypothesis that long after its publication the belief persisted that the agents of disease were airborne poisons or "miasmas" generated spontaneously either in chambers beneath the earth's surface or in fetid places above. Above ground, the miasma-producing ingredients were thought to be warm air, moisture, and decaying animal and vegetable matter. Unhealthy places, therefore, were hot and humid; healthy ones cool and dry. Medicine had not advanced since the days of Champlain.

Unable to identify the causes of disease, physicians were at a loss to prescribe treatment other than to recommend a change of air. Thus the rich, in the fever season, retreated to high ground or the seaside where they breathed pure, well-ventilated air and drank, or bathed in, health-giving waters. By the middle of the last century few responsible physicians had any faith in conventional medicine. "Every practical physician," wrote the admirable Mississippi Valley physician Daniel Drake, "is aware of the frequent failure of all kinds of medication ... and of the great value of cool and fresh air ... united with active exercise ... new scenery, *and the disuse of all medicine.*" A century earlier William Douglass, an equally sceptical American physician, had remarked "[that] more die of the practitioner than the natural course of the disease."

Seasonal movements to avoid tropical heat and its all too frequent concomitants, malaria and yellow fever, began in the 1760s when rich planters from the South and the West Indies sailed to Newport and Cape May, and occasionally to Quebec City and Montreal. Heat, humidity and stagnant waters were not, by themselves, the generators of disease but they were conditions much loved by the yellow fever bacillus and the anopheles, or malaria-carrying, mosquito. By the middle of the 19th century a movement that had begun as a trickle became a trek. In the years before the Civil War about fifty thousand southerners summered either on the Atlantic coast or in inland resorts in the Appalachians, the Alleghenies, and the Ozarks. By 1857 the big Saratoga hotels could accommodate twelve hundred guests each.

From Newport and Cape May, summer escapees from the cities in the south worked their way up the Atlantic coast. By the late 1860s they had reached Mt Desert Island and Bar Harbor, and by the 1870s they were on the threshold of the coolest coast of all: the shores of the Bay of Fundy.

THE CAMPOBELLO COMPANY ↬

FRUSTRATED IN HIS EFFORTS to keep Campobello out of Confederation, in 1872 Captain Robinson-Owen decided to sell the island, or at least those parts of it still in leasehold. A stagnant American money market and protracted negotiations with prospective buyers delayed the sale, but in 1881 title to the Owen lands passed to the Campobello Land Company, a syndicate of businessmen from Boston and New York. With New World acumen the company lifted all restrictions on the sale of land, encouraging fishermen, farmers and tradesmen to buy outright if they cared to, and if they did not, or could not, to make semi-annual or quarterly payments.

Within a few years the company had built three hotels: The Owen, Ty'n-y-Coed, and Ty'n-y-maes, all on former Owen properties. All three prospered until about 1910. Guests arrived by steamship from Boston and Portland or took the train to St Stephen and completed the journey on a steamer down the St Croix. Steamship passengers left Boston at eight in the morning, arrived in Portland at six on the same day, and in Eastport at nine the following morning.

Campobello's beauty aside, the chief selling point of the island was the healthfulness of its cool and, measured by relative humidity, dry climate. The attractiveness of the climate had no less a champion than General A.W. Greely of the US Signal Corps, an acclaimed explorer, geographer and climatologist. In a *Scribner's* article, "Where Shall We Spend Our Summer?" General Greely recommended two towns for their near-perfect summer climates: San Diego and Eastport, Campobello's neighbour. On General Greely's chart of relative humidity, Passamaquoddy lay in one of the driest belts.

Support for the therapeutic qualities of Campobello's climate came from academic as well as military quarters. In a report on the island, prepared for the Campobello Co. in 1881, Professor N.S. Shaler of Harvard presented a view of the ideal climate that was even more fastidious than General Greely's. The Rockies and the West (including California and San Diego) he dismissed as a treeless waterless waste subject to extremes of temperature; the North was an incubator for mosquitoes; and the Mississippi valley, the South, and the Atlantic coast south of Rhode Island, where floodplains and bayous lay "festering" in the hot sun, were seats of miasmatic fevers. Even southern New England, plagued by southwest winds as debilitating and fever-ridden as those of the Mississippi valley, failed to qualify. Only on the coast of Maine was the sojourner comfortable and safe. And even here only in three localities were there acceptable combinations of climate and scenery: Camden, at the mouth of the Penobscot, Mt Desert, and Passamaquoddy Bay.

At all three places, northern currents and strong tides cooled the waters and freshened the air. By day, the air at Campobello was, in Professor Shaler's phrase, as pure as that of a ship's deck; at night, when filtered through "extensive forests" of balsamic firs, it was a soporific. The pungent yet soothing aroma of the firs, asserted the Professor, quieted the nervous system and invited sleep. The proof of the pudding was the condition of the islanders. Despite their hard labour and "scant" diet, Campobello fisherfolk were "the best conditioned people" he had ever seen, and their children the very "models of vigour and health."

The hotels, naturally, took up the appealing refrain, their brochures promising "soft yet bracing air" and "absolute relief" from the allergens that cause hay fever. The connection between pollens and hayfever had only recently been discovered—in the early 1870s—and, there being no antihistamines, swollen sinuses often spelled misery. Even fog, that could be persistent on the island, was turned to advantage. In no time at all, wrote J.G. Lorimer, a well-known local journalist and newspaper owner, the visitor learned to revel in it as in sunshine, "becoming as sportive as a lamb on its island home, or the tumbling porpoise in the bay." Visitors were almost as effusive. Edward A. Silsbee regarded fog as a "gentle restorative for an overstrung race:" whereas dry continental air excited the senses, fog-filled air was "sedative and sympathetic."

In addition to building hotels, the Campobello Co. sold land for summer houses. Professors Dean and Shaler of Harvard College laid out a subdivision of some 800 acres, divided into two to six acre lots, near the Ty'n-y-Coed hotel.

Gazebos or small pavilions for enjoying views of the water or the garden were standard appendages of fashionable summer houses. In times that are more active than contemplative many have been left to moulder. This one is in the grounds of a house on Campobello.

Among the buyers of company land were James and Sara Delano Roosevelt, parents of the one-year-old Franklin, who in 1883 were guests at Ty'n-y-Coed. Instead of a subdivision lot they bought ten acres from the company on a brow overlooking Friar's Bay and on it built a fifteen room house. James Roosevelt was then vice president of the Delaware and Hudson Railway.

St Andrews and the C.P.R. ∂

St Andrews developed in ways similar to Campobello. In 1888, a syndicate of American and Canadian businessmen floated the St Andrews Land Company and bought choice parcels of land in and around the town. Sir Leonard Tilley was the company's first president and Sir Donald Smith, a founder of the Canadian Pacific Railway, one of its early directors. The Americans were mostly Bostonians with railroad and steamship connections. On one of its parcels of land the company built a model summer house, in the

Roosevelt Cottage, the centrepiece of the International Park. The four satellite cottages house participants in the Park Commission's Conference Programme.

St Andrews, from the harbour, nestling beneath the turrets and towers of the Algonquin Hotel.

picturesque Queen Anne style, which it hoped would set the tone for future development. On another parcel, atop the low hill that crowns the site of the town, it built a large summer hotel, the Algonquin. A stone's throw from the Algonquin lay empty Fort Tipperary, built in 1812 to repulse the very nation on which its new neighbour would depend. To complete the irony, the old barracks was used to house waitresses and chambermaids who in fine weather entertained friends and family on the grassy redoubts.

The Algonquin, flying both the Union Jack and the Stars and Stripes,

opened with a flourish in late June, 1889. In attendance were the Governor
General of Canada and the Governor of Maine. Most of the guests arrived by
special trains, one of which was a Pullman coach that left Boston in the morning
and arrived in St Andrews in the evening. Other Boston guests left home in the
evening and arrived at noon the following day. The nautically inclined came by
sea. Owners of private yachts sailed directly up the coast, while others took a
steamer from Boston to Eastport and transferred to a local service for the twelve
mile crossing of Passamaquoddy Bay.

In its report on the hotel, the *Boston Home Journal* found the
appointments first class and of the kind that well-to-do Americans then
considered indispensable. The building, "liberally piazzered, gabled and turreted,"
it described as "Old English" in style and with "a view that can hardly be
surpassed on the coast." The town, on the other hand, fell short of the standards
set by the hotel: "the ruins of a once lively shipping port now passed into a
dream." But what it lacked materially, it made up for in charm. The combination
of old, unpainted buildings, and inhabitants who were "simple" and "all fond of
flowers" added up to an atmosphere that, in spite of the nearness of the United
States, was "quaint," "old country," and "distinctly foreign."

Although Boston money and Yankee enterprise were critical to the
development of the town as a resort, railways also brought St Andrews within the
orbit of Montreal, then the richest city in Canada. In 1889, the C.P.R. acquired
both the New Brunswick and Quebec Railway, which connected St Andrews with
central Canada, and the European and North American Railway that linked
Boston and Bangor, Maine, with Saint John, New Brunswick. The lines crossed at
the remote, workaday lumber town of McAdam where, to accommodate
passengers switching to or from the St Andrews branch line, the C.P.R. built a
massive station hotel in its turreted chateau style. The station still stands, but
with passenger trains down to three a week from sixteen a day at the height of the
season at the beginning of the century, it ranks as southern New Brunswick's best
known folly. Passenger service ended in December 1994.

A fashionable resort reachable overnight from Montreal inevitably

Sir William Van Horne's shingled silo and his turreted three-storey barn where, so it is said, white-coated workers attended to his Dutch belted cattle.

attracted C.P.R. executives and shareholders. First to arrive was Sir William Van Horne, builder of the railway and then its president. In 1891 Van Horne bought the southern end of a small offshore island (Minister's Island) where he designed and built a twenty-eight room mansion house. To honour his father—Cornelius Covenhoven Van Horne—and acknowledge his Dutch ancestry, he named it Covenhoven. Van Horne turned most of the 160 acre property into a self-contained experimental farm. He built a plant to produce carbide gas for lighting and cooking, and extensive greenhouses to start his flowers, vegetables, fruit trees and shrubs. Water came from a well with a purpose built windmill. The centrepiece of the farm was a massive barn, three storeys high, with turreted silos, a shingled roof with flared gable ends, a freight elevator, and two floors kept pin-neat for Sir William's coveted Dutch-belted cattle. Workers in the barns wore long white lab coats, and at the end of each day they were required to spread fresh sawdust on the floors.

A planner and builder, rather than an operator, the restless Van Horne spent relatively little time at "Covenhoven," but the estate was the family's summer home for twenty-five years. The Van Hornes arrived in late June in Sir William's personal C.P.R. coach, *The Saskatchewan,* and disembarked at a small station built at one end of a bar that, at ebb tide, connected Minister's Island with the mainland. With the family came a full complement of servants (chauffer, hostler, housemen, butler, cooks, maids and a nurse) as well as Sir William's carriages and horses.

Where Van Horne led, other C.P.R. executives and shareholders inevitably followed. In 1902, Sir Thomas Shaughnessy, Van Horne's able successor as president of the railway, built a large summer house on the site of old Fort Tipperary beside the Algonquin Hotel. Five years later the C.P.R. acquired the Algonquin and with it the holdings of the St Andrews Land Company. Fire destroyed the original hotel in 1914, but within a year the C.P.R. had raised a new, fire-resistant building on the same site.

As owner of the Algonquin and much of the southern tip of the peninsula, the C.P.R. automatically took over the promotion of the town. Two attributes were stressed: the healthfulness of the climate and the many opportunities for outdoor recreation. With public confidence in conventional medicine still at a low ebb, the C.P.R., like the owners of the first Algonquin, played on the themes of climate and health. By the end of the century, fresh air and exercise, physical hygiene and general temperance were middle-class cults.

St Andrews offered health-conscious vacationers "invigorating" sea water and air tempered by contact with the "sounding" sea. As in Campobello, the air was filtered through relaxing and sleep-inducing stands of balsam fir. St Andrews, too, was a place where people with weak lungs or an inclination to allergies could breathe deeply and easily. Protected by the buffer of islands at the mouth of the

Covenhoven and Minister's Island, seen from Indian Point, St Andrews. On the shore to the right of the main building is a bathing house.

Bay, it was spared the worst of the cool but nevertheless—as C.P.R. advertisers reassured visitors—complexion-improving Fundy fogs. Like Campobello, St Andrews was also a refuge from hayfever, a malady, as then perceived, of well-to-do Anglo-Saxons. Working folk, and country people in particular, were thought to be immune. With no antidote available, the most effective way of getting relief was to breathe pollen-free sea breezes.

St Andrews hoteliers were quick to to take advantage of a fashionable disability. Word of the town's pollen-free status quickly reached the American Hayfever Association, which placed St Andrews on the agenda of one of its first annual meetings. In anticipation of a rush of "weeping-eyed sufferers," as the *Beacon* described them, St Andrews hoteliers announced in 1888 that they were preparing to stay open until the first of October, the effective end of the hayfever season.

St Andrews and Campobello also profited from neurasthenia, a nervous condition that, like hayfever, was also associated with the urban rich. But unlike hayfever, which had detectable physical symptoms, neurasthenia's were difficult to pin down. Sufferers complained of malaise and a loss of energy and ambition that their physicians attributed to the tensions of a high-flying city life. A century earlier, Europeans with similar symptoms (the condition was known as *Europamudigkeit,* or sickness with Europe or civilization) escaped to the American West, then a wilderness. But with the West largely settled, and rest rather than adventure the prescribed antidote, late 19th century Americans escaped to quiet resorts in the east. Most neurasthenics were from the cities of New England and the Atlantic seaboard.

For most health and comfort conscious vacationers, however, the chief attraction of St Andrews was that, like most places on the Fundy coast, it was virtually mosquito free. Malaria, caused not by bad air but, as the bacteriologist Sir Ronald Ross had demonstrated in 1895, the bite of female mosquitos, was still endemic in the interior and southern parts of the continent. Nor, too, as "Mabel" of the St Andrews *Beacon* was fond of reminding her readers, was it unknown on the Riviera. At Nice, she wrote in one of her more impish "French Letters," the mosquitoes hummed as loudly as hand organs and were so aggressive that an Italian Duke, staying at a nearby castle, was known to wear armour to ward them off. Nice was also a "nice" place for wind as well as mosquitoes. On six days of the week, vacationers had to contend with the mistral, a cold wind from the Alps that funneled down the Rhone Valley, and on the seventh day with the Sirocco from the Sahara.

Although St Andrews was not a spa in the European sense, any resort worthy of the name had to be able to offer healing waters. Some were found in a convenient spring behind the Algonquin, covered with a portico to give them classical authority, and then named "Algonquin Springs." The spring water, said to have been sought out by Indians in the 16th and 17th centuries, is supposed to have alleviated rheumatism and dyspepsia. By 1914, medicine had made enough progress that sea water was no longer drunk as a cure for gout, gonorrhea, and worms, as it had been in Europe well into the 19th century, but sea-water bathing was still considered therapeutic. Guests not up to braving the waters of the Bay could bathe in tepid water piped into their bathtubs from a sea-fed, but partly enclosed, cove behind the hotel.

The town's amenities for outdoor recreation needed no boosting. There were scenic walks and drives, good fishing in the Bay and nearby lakes and streams, and croquet, tennis, lawn bowling and golf. Croquet was conducive to summer flirtations and, like tennis and golf, it allowed women to exercise freely without any loss of decorum. "Golf fever," according to *Harper's Monthly,* began raging in the 1890s, and for the afflicted in St Andrews there was a nine hole course on an elevated stretch of shoreline below the Algonquin. Yachtsmen could run before the wind in Passamaquoddy Bay, and to lure them there the C.P.R. billed St Andrews as the "Newport of the North," pointing out that the town bore the same relationship to the St Croix River and Passamaquoddy Bay as Newport News to the James River and Hampton Roads.

For unspecialized vacationers, the C.P.R. coined the jingle "St Andrews by-the-Sea" and, always ready to marry commerce and art, commissioned George Horne Russell, a well-known Canadian landscape painter, to paint views of the town for its posters and advertising brochures. Horne Russell, too, became another of St Andrews' celebrated summer residents.

Unlike some of the New England resorts, St Andrews never became a painter's colony, even though eminently paintable and attractive to painters. Van Horne, who was a talented amateur painter and an astute collector, occasionally painted with George Inness, the American landscape painter. Inness's son built a summer house near the first Algonquin Hotel and for a few seasons before his death in 1894, Inness senior visited the town. One September afternoon, when painting on a rock on the beach at Minister's Island, he almost hastened that death. Oblivious to a fast-rising tide, he might have been carried off had his wife not alerted him to the danger.

So attractive was the town and so successful the C.P.R.'s promotion of it that by the beginning of this century St Andrews was one of the northeast's most fashionable resorts. Visitors with means stayed at the Algonquin, sometimes for the entire season, or they built summer houses on the high ground near the hotel or along choice parts of the shore. About a dozen of the houses were designed by Edward Maxwell, the prominent Montreal architect. Maxwell had come to St Andrews in 1898 to correct problems with Van Horne's original design of Covenhoven, add an extension, and design the wonderfully ornate barn. He also designed the station at McAdam. Attracted by St Andrews, he bought, at Van Horne's suggestion, five acres of choice shoreland across from Minister's Island and built a summer house for himself and his young family.

Most of Maxwell's St Andrews houses were built in the American "shingle" style, which is to say they were grand houses made

In St Andrews, summer houses were built on the hill adjacent to the Algonquin Hotel or along choice parts of the shore. George Horne Russell, the celebrated painter, chose a shore site. Like several other well-known landscape painters, Russell painted advertising posters for the C.P.R.

to look appealingly accidental and picturesque. Maxwell apprenticed from 1888-1892 with the Boston architects (Shepley, Rutan & Coolidge) who had taken over the practice of Henry Hobson Richardson, one of the most influential 19th century architects. In an attempt to escape what he regarded as the inhibiting regularity of classical or Renaissance styles, Richardson had experimented with new domestic designs in the 1870s and 1880s. Taking the English Queen Anne style as his point of departure, he created interiors that were free flowing, light-filled and connected— through French doors, verandas and porches—with the outdoors.

Richardson's exteriors were also distinctive. His houses were capped by long roofs and, as one writer put it, almost medieval arrangements of dormers, chimneys and gables. All wooden exterior surfaces, including supporting pillars, were covered with rough shingles. Though inspired by English Gothic and Queen Anne styles, the shingle style was truly American: the first to reflect American materials and techniques, the American sense of space, and the conditions of American life.

In St Andrews, as elsewhere along the Atlantic coast, the informality of vacation life prompted architects to accentuate the characteristics of the shingle style. Living and dining rooms were usually combined and they opened onto verandas, patios, and lawns and gardens that were treated as extensions of the living space. Prevailing garden styles, as in the Maine resorts, were a combination of Italianate and English picturesque, formal terraces and flower beds rubbing shoulders with naturalistic arrangements of lawns, planted trees and shrubs. Several of them were laid out by well-known landscape architects, among them Frederick G. Todd of Montreal who designed the setting for the Saskatchewan Legislative Building in Regina. The building itself was designed by Edward and William Maxwell.

As settings for outdoor living, games, and frequent entertainments, the gardens were invariably fenced and in winter, if the property had gates, padlocked. Downslope in the old town, yards for the most part were—as many still are—open and unfenced. In pioneer villages and towns, if there were no marauding animals to keep out, fences and gates that signalled the Old World

One of Edward Maxwell's "fun" houses, Hillcrest, designed (with his brother William) for the C.P.R. executive C.R. Hosmer in 1905. The covering of shingles, and the turrets and steeply pitched roofs, were reminders that though grand, the house was merely a summer one. But in breaking the classical Georgian mould on American architecture, the effect of the irregular and seemingly playful details was profound.

sense of property were considered unneighbourly.

The summer, or "fun houses" as Maxwell described them, form a decorative horseshoe around the town's workaday, colonial core. In keeping with their function they were given romantic and sometimes playful names: *Berwick Brae, Clibrig, Les Goelands, Tillietudlem, Pansy Patch.* Their owners arrived in late June with an entourage of maids, cooks, horsemen (later chauffers) and, in some cases, butlers. To prepare for their arrival the unpaved and usually dusty streets were watered down, public places tidied, and the town band tuned and readied to welcome any dignitaries that might be among them.

For about forty years St Andrews drew the rich and the powerful like moths to a flame. Insulated by wealth and social distance, they savoured for a few

In parts of the old town, lawns, gardens and even cemeteries run together as if in one common property. In earlier days, fences—if not needed to keep out animals—and other badges of ownership were considered unneighbourly.

months each summer the class, or even caste, privileges that were theirs in the cities. As in Campobello and the Maine resorts, hotel guests and "cottagers" were overwhelmingly Anglo Saxon and Protestant. But by 1920 St Andrews' days as an exclusive resort were numbered. The model T and rising standards of living brought the Algonquin and other fashionable resorts well within physical and financial range of the middle classes. St Andrews remained popular but the new, mobile vacationers no longer stayed at the Algonquin for a month or a season. Descendants of the original owners of summer houses, however, tended to stay on and many have done so down to the fourth and fifth generation. Many, too, by taking up permanent residence have become part of the social fabric of the town.

More than a century of admiring attention has inevitably affected the look and feel of St Andrews. Like any pedigreed resort, the town is very well groomed. It is also exceptionally well preserved. An isolated, peninsular location may have been a merchant's nightmare but it is a preservationist's idyll. Abandoned by trade and industry, St Andrews remained fixed in the amber of its mid-19th century depression. Not only were old buildings preserved, but no new ones were built in a period—the late Victorian—now considered the nadir of Canadian architecture. While the main streets of Canada were being lined with facades bereft of proportion, liveliness, and charm, and built of a brick that would never mellow, Water Street slumbered. In recent times, government and a supermarket chain have made up some of the late 19th century's losses,

Craft studios enliven the landscape of leisure. This fine Eastport Cape, built sometime before 1850, is now the home and workshop of a woodcarver.

but despite these lapses Water Street in St Andrews remains one of the most attractive main streets in the country.

Once St Andrews became a resort, its preservation was assured in spite of the absence of protective by-laws. The town's face was its fortune and merchants, hoteliers and astute property owners had a vested interest in seeing that it continued to age gracefully. Historic resorts are inherently conservative. Families and summer residents who returned year after year also resisted change. The one landscape we all cherish and would like to preserve in fact as well as memory is the summer landscape of childhood.

GRAND MANAN ♪

TOURISM IS ALSO IMPORTANT TO DEER ISLAND, Eastport and Grand Manan but its touch has been lighter than in St Andrews and Campobello. There is in each the usual sprinkling of restaurants, motels, and guesthouses, and each summer there is an influx of people who own property on the islands, but there are no resorts. Deer Island and Grand Manan, which have to be sought out, pride themselves on appealing to travellers and sojourners who present no threat to the even tenor of their ways. Accessible only by ferry, and notably lacking in anything that might be described as "attractions" or "amusements," they draw the naturalist, the walker, the historian, the painter and the contemplative.

The least accessible island, and therefore the most alluring, is Grand Manan. One of its earliest visitors also happened to be one of the most notable: John James Audubon, the great naturalist and illustrator. In May 1833, he sailed to Whitehead Island on a revenue cutter to verify reports of a remarkable change in the behaviour of herring gulls. The gulls were breeding in great numbers and visibly adapting to a new predator: sailors and fishermen who collected their eggs from nests on or near the shore. To escape the attentions of the predators some of the gulls, much to Audubon's astonishment, had begun nesting in spruce trees— in high branches on the exposed edge of the woods but at heights of only eight to

Shucked scallop shells lining the Ross Island thoroughfare—an
undersea road that connects Ross Island and Grand Manan.

ten feet in the secluded centre. The sight of broad-winged birds threading their way through the trees to reach their nests had, he intimated, to be seen to be believed.

Since Audubon's day, naturalists and people of kindred spirit have been arriving in ever increasing, but not threatening, numbers. Whales and dolphins occasionally cavort near the shore and birds, including the elusive puffin, nest by the hundreds of thousands on the outer and uninhabited islands. Painters attracted by the powerful and spectacular in nature came to paint the cliffs, seas, and sunsets. The most famous of them was Frederick Church of the Hudson River School, painter of icebergs, erupting volcanoes, tropical rainforests and, in the summer of 1877, the cliffs at North Head. Painters of the Hudson River School had discovered Bar Harbor and Mount Desert Island in the 1840s.

For painters with tastes more picturesque than sublime there were the fishing villages where, as one susceptible visitor put it, "everything appears to have been arranged for artistic effect. The old boats, the tumble-down storehouses, the picturesque costumes, the breaking surf, and all the miscellaneous paraphernalia of such a place [Sprague's Cove, North Head], set off as they are by the noble background of richly colored cliffs, produce an effect that is as rare as beautiful."

Grand Manan could always be reached by fishing vessels or mail packets from Eastport. Visitors came to Eastport either by train or by "Boston" boat and then "caught a sail" or took the mail packet. By 1875 there was a summer steamboat service with the mainland and by 1882 a summer ferry on a route that included Campobello, Eastport and Bar Harbor. Early in the 1880s the Grand Manan Steamboat Company, floated on local capital, bought an American steamer and in 1884 inaugurated the first regular, year-round ferry service with the mainland.

Visitors then stayed for weeks at a time, at first boarding in private houses then in hotels and guest houses built specifically for summer visitors. In 1879 two Boston men bought land to build a hotel above the spectacular cliffs at Southern Head but the site and location were more romantic than practical and the hotel never materialized. Far more feasible was an inn (the Marble Head) at North Head opened by Capt James Pettes and now operating as the Marathon Hotel.

Visitors took pride in roughing it and in having found a quiet backwater away from the main tourist streams. The most illustrious escapee was the novelist Willa Cather. She made her first visit in the summer of 1922, travelling by train from New York to Lubec, then by ferry to Campobello and steamboat to Grand Manan. Extremely private, she referred to the island only once (in the story "Before Breakfast" published a year after her death in 1947) and then in terms that would not attract her readers. Her summer haunt was "that bit of wooded rock in the sea" hardly on the map and "known only to the motor launches that called after a catch of herring." To reach it meant braving "the cast off coaches of liquidated railroads" and the "two worst boats in the world." Only the climate, so damp that she had to dry her Lucky Strikes before a fire, was spared.

For three years, until 1926, she and her companion Edith Lewis stayed in a cottage on a converted farmstead, "Orchardside," overlooking Whale Cove Bay. Then, in 1927, they built their own cottage, to a classic Cape Cod design, about a quarter of a mile away and connected to the main complex by an old wagon road through the woods. "The cabin modestly squatted on a tiny clearing between a tall spruce and the sea—sat about fifty yards back from the edge of the red sandstone cliff which dropped some two hundred feet to a ... beach so narrow that it was covered at high tide." Until driven away by the threat posed by German submarines patrolling in the Bay of Fundy, Willa Cather and Edith Lewis spent fourteen consecutive summers on the island. Several of Cather's novels were written there, including her last, *Sapphira and the Slave Girl,* finished in September 1940, the year of the final visit.

FIVE

AQUACULTURE AND THE MARINE ENVIRONMENT

When the Loyalist transports from Castine anchored in St Andrews harbour on October 3, 1783, the tide was at the ebb. Passengers and crews began unloading on the beach. It is said that during the course of the day they had to move their belongings three times to protect them from the rising waters of the flood tide. At Castine the tide is a respectable ten feet, but at St Andrews it is twenty-eight feet and in the Minas Basin, at the head of the Bay of Fundy, an outrageous forty-eight.

Although some of the details of the enormous displacement have yet to be worked out, the general mechanism now seems clear. When water in a basin is set in motion it moves back and forth at regular intervals and if, as in the Bay of Fundy and the Gulf of Maine—which is a geological basin—it is joined by another body of water oscillating with roughly the same rhythm the displacement is intensified. In physics, the effect is known as resonance. At twelve hour intervals, water moving back and forth within the Bay and the Gulf is reinforced by tidal (lunar-generated) north Atlantic water sweeping down from Georges Bank and around the corner of south-west Nova Scotia. In the Bay of Fundy resonance gets a helping hand from topography; as the water moves up the Bay it is increasingly confined by the narrow, funneling shape and the shelving bottom.

If there are still lingering doubts over the precise causes of the tides, there is nothing enigmatic about their effects. Twice each day, in the lower Bay of Fundy, about a cubic mile of water flows into and out of Passamaquoddy Bay. Were the movement unimpeded, it would be no more than the dramatic filling and emptying of a natural basin. But the islands plugging the mouth of the Bay convert movements that might otherwise be no more than strong flows into powerful eddies and maelstroms that have long enticed engineers and intrigued ecologists. The "Old Sow," a great whirlpool between Eastport and Deer Island driven by currents that flow around the island and through the Lubec/Campobello channel, is one of the world's largest.

For engineers, the attraction of the tidal flows lies in the energy latent in millions of tons of water muscling their way through the narrow channels between the islands. The idea of closing the gaps between the islands, damming up the floodtide water, and channeling it through turbines at the ebb occurred first to Wallace R. Turnbull, the Saint John inventor of the pitched-prop propellor. In 1919, he and Dexter P. Cooper, an American engineer with Campobello connections, designed a double basin scheme, using both

At flood tide, these mounds of rockweed fronds on Grand Manan rise to create an underwater thicket that provides cover for countless creatures, including young fish. Harvesting rockweed for chemical extracts and fertilizer has disturbed both environmentalists and fishermen.

Passamaquoddy and Cobscook bays, that would cross the international boundary. Work on what was to be a series of experimental dams began in 1935 but in spite of presidential support the scheme, dogged by financial and political difficulties, had to be abandoned. Yet the dream of harnessing the Passamaquoddy tides has never died. The US Army Corps of Engineers re-evaluated the scheme in the 1950s, the 1960s and the 1970s, rejecting it each time on grounds of cost, not practicability.

For naturalists and biologists, interest in the massive displacements of water lies in their climatic and ecological effects. The great tidal range exposes, at

Tidal pools at Indian Point, St Andrews, are magnets for naturalists and marine biologists. The shore nearby was the base for Canada's first (moveable) marine science and fisheries laboratory.

low tide, broad stretches of rocky shore with their distinct flora and fauna. The ebbing tide leaves exposed, or stranded on the beach and in small rock pools, a remarkable variety of seaweeds and small animals, all adapted to the cold waters of the Bay. The riches, as Dr Joseph Stafford, one of the first curators of the St Andrews Biological Station, remarked, are inescapable: "Turn what way he will an observer is likely to come upon the common star-fish in many colour varieties, the sea-urchin and the sea-cucumber, among echinoderms. The Mollusca [mussels, clams, periwinkles] are abundantly represented ... *Nereis, Arenicola* (etc.) are common representatives of the worms; while crabs, hermit crabs, barnacles and sand-hoppers are the commonest types of Crustacea. A good many hydroids, Polyzoa and sponges may also be easily procured along the shore." In Passamaquoddy the intertidal zone is as rich in species as the subtidal one.

Climatically, the chief effect of the tides is to cool the shores of the Bay and the islands. Water upwelling from sunless depths reinforces the cold delivered by the south-striking Labrador and coastal Nova Scotia currents. Even in summer, night time temperatures seldom rise above 10°C (50°F), and because they often fall to the dew point, fog is frequent. The result is a sub Arctic shore biota, or boreal coast, in a region exactly mid-way between the equator and the Poles.

Within the ocean itself the effects of the upwellings are even more dramatic. As tidal water sweeps around the bend of southwestern Nova Scotia and approaches Passamaquoddy's tangle of islands and submerged ledges, cold, nutrient-rich water is pumped up from the dark seafloor into the light, or photic zone. At the surface, microscopic sea plants, or phytoplankton, use sunlight to convert into food (simple sugars) the nitrates and other minerals brought to the surface by the upwellings. Phytoplankton, which lie on the surface like a pale greenish-brown carpet, are the first link in the food chain of the oceans. On them feed zooplankton, minute sea animals which are the staple diet for the juveniles and adults of most marine creatures.

In places where tidal water has to force its way over ledges and through constricted channels between the islands, eddies concentrate the carpet of zooplankton in amounts thick enough to attract not only fish but whales, porpoises and dolphins. Also to the feast come gulls, ospreys (fish hawks), cormorants and bald eagles that feed on herring and whatever else they can kill or carry away. Even creatures that never leave the ocean floor benefit from the great stirrings; the movement of the water stimulates the plant and marine life that supports bottom dwelling invertebrates such as lobsters (crustaceans) and scallops (molluscs).

MARINE BIOLOGY AND FISHERIES RESEARCH ⌁

AN ECOSYSTEM THAT IS AS RICH and varied as any on the eastern seaboard, or for that matter on almost any other seaboard, proved irresistible to biologists engaged in marine and fisheries research. The first group arrived in the summer of 1898, working from a moveable laboratory—a fifty-foot long wooden building shaped like a Pullman car—that could be loaded onto a scow. For two years it lay above high water on the eastern shore of Indian Point, St Andrews, and was then towed to various locations in Nova Scotia, Prince Edward Island and the Gaspé Peninsula of Quebec.

In 1906, when the Federal Government decided to create a permanent, year-round biological station in aid of the fisheries, St Andrews was virtually the automatic choice of location. There was some competition from Chester, in Nova Scotia, but the greater richness and diversity of Passamaquoddy's flora and fauna, and its local fishery, left the selection committee with little choice. The Chester and Nova Scotia fleets fished, for the most part, on the Grand Banks and their catches went directly to the Boston market, or if brought home they were already barreled for shipment. Few fish were taken in local waters.

To a local fishery and the riches of the Bay, St Andrews could add excellent rail connections with Montreal and Boston, fish weirs from which material could easily be collected, and sheltered waters of varying depths. Through Sir Thomas Shaughnessy and the St Andrews Land Company—a

Sir Thomas Tait's summer house, Links Crest, now a residence for the Huntsman Marine Science Centre, looks onto Passamaquoddy Bay across the fairways of the Algonquin Hotel golf course. Sir Thomas was private secretary to Sir William Van Horne. The house was designed by Edward Maxwell.

subsidiary of the C.P.R. of which Sir Thomas Shaughnessy was then president—St Andrews could also offer shore land at nominal cost: a three-and-a-half acre site at Brandy, or Smuggler's Cove, a secluded inlet just outside the town at the mouth of the St Croix.

The Department of Fisheries and Oceans Biological Station at St Andrews—simply "the Station" to townspeople—is now one of a trio of marine research institutions in or near the town. In response to a perceived need for closer cooperation between government and university researchers, in the late 1960s a sister institution—the Huntsman Marine Science Centre—was built on a shore site adjacent to the Biological Station. Dr A.G. Hunstman, eponym for the new centre, was the first full-time director of the Biological Station and one of Canada's most distinguished marine biologists. The Huntsman was an immediate success and to meet the need for more staff and visitors quarters, the New Brunswick Government provided funds for the purchase of an adjoining estate: the former summer residence of Sir Thomas Tait. Sir Thomas was Secretary to Sir William Van Horne. The Tait house and estate, just up the hill from the Huntsman's shore quarters, is the "upper campus."

Supported by its membership, which includes government, private and corporate sponsors, and a dozen universities, Huntsman's complex of laboratories and residences and its thirty-five or so permanent staff are now host to marine scientists from Canada, the United States and Europe, and to groups of students from its affiliated universities. One of these is the University of Maine. Huntsman staff, too, conduct research in their own right, and in conjunction with the Biological Station the Huntsman operates the Atlantic Reference Centre (ARC), a remarkable species library and identification centre.

ARC began as a more or less random assortment of plant and animal life taken from the Bay, but a determined and systematic programme of collection, identification and classification has converted it into a comprehensive collection of the ichthyoplankton (fish in the larval stage) of the entire continental, or Scotian shelf. ARC now houses examples of both the eggs and larvae and adult forms of the fish and invertebrates—shellfish, sponges, worms, etc.—that live in the coastal waters and estuaries of the North Atlantic between Baffin Island and Cape Cod. As both a major repository for marine and estuarine biota, and a species identification and taxonomic centre of some renown, ARC doubles as a research and advisory centre and a resource for marine scientists around the world.

In keeping with its mandate to establish links between government and universities, and to disseminate information on marine life and the marine environment to as wide an audience as possible, the Huntsman also embarked on a programme of public education. Staff go out to the schools and the schools

come to the Huntsman. Teachers from all parts of Canada, a dozen states, England, Scandinavia, and even Asia, have taken in-service training while students do both field work and—crucial to the study of marine biology—hands-on laboratory work. In summer, visitors are invited to a museum/aquarium where, in imaginative and attractive displays, they can see examples of many of the organisms that live in the waters of the Quoddy region. For the young there is a "touch pool" where species can be handled, and for the young of all ages there are a couple of engaging harbour seals who for a few pailfuls of herring turn mealtimes into public performances.

Dr. Gerry Friars, chief scientist of the Salmon Genetics Research Programme at the Atlantic Salmon Federation, inspecting salmon fry growing in tanks at the Chamcook headquarters. By supplying smolts to fish farmers, the Federation's role in the development of aquaculture was critical. The netting is to discourage the attentions of kingfishers, ospreys and seagulls.

The third, and most recent, member of what is, in effect, a family of fisheries research and teaching institutions is the Atlantic Salmon Federation.

Seeking a more central location on the north east coast, the Federation—or the International Atlantic Salmon Foundation as it was in 1971—moved from its makeshift quarters on the Gaspé Peninsula to St Andrews. Its first home in St Andrews—an office provided by the Biological Station—was also temporary, but in 1974 the Federation moved into its own newly-built quarters on Chamcook Bay a few miles outside the town. With a permanent staff of about forty, the Federation, to the delight of sport-fishermen on several continents, dedicates itself to the well-being of the Atlantic salmon.

Jointly with the Huntsman and the Department of Fisheries and Oceans, it conducts research in genetics and selective breeding, undertakes environmental management schemes, campaigns against illegal fishing and indiscriminate commercial

Banks of salmon cages at the mouth of Harbour de Loutre, Campobello. In the background is Wilson's Beach.

fishing, and carries out an extensive programme of public education. At the Chamcook headquarters is a visitor centre which, by incorporating part of Chamcook Creek, shows the salmon in its natural habitat. At Chamcook, too, are produced the Federation's two magazines, *Salar,* the Atlantic salmon newsletter and the *Atlantic Salmon Journal.* The Federation has individual or corporate members in all ten Canadian provinces, fifty US states, and thirty-one countries.

AQUACULTURE ᧓

RESEARCH AT ALL THREE MARINE AND fisheries establishments is both pure and applied, but as wild fish stocks decline to unprecedented levels and pressure on the survivors mounts, more and more of the applied research is directed at aquaculture, or fish farming. The plight of the wild fishery is common knowledge. Waters that once were alive with fish are now, by historical standards, empty. Vessels equipped with sonar and radar equipment for detecting the schools, with large and efficient nets for scooping them up, and powerful hydraulic systems for hauling the nets in, chase fewer and fewer prey.

Few doubt that overfishing is the chief cause of the decline but natural population cycles, industrial pollution, the cooling of the Labrador current, and changing patterns of fish migration may well be others. But whatever the precise mix of causes, there is no denying their effects; both scientists and fishermen now speak resignedly of the collapse of groundfish stocks. The survival of the northern cod, the very name for fish in some languages, may now be in question. In Passamaquoddy, as in most inshore localities, haddock and pollock as well as cod are fading into folk memory, and even the remarkably prolific herring may be in short supply.

Intensive trapping, digging and gathering have also affected the numbers of shellfish. Twenty years ago, when few people were digging, clams were plentiful. But rising prices, hard times, and a rash of amateur diggers have severely reduced populations. Coastal development, too, by contaminating estuaries and intertidal flats with fecal matter has led to the closure of many beds. Lobsters, which are still caught by the old method of baiting traps, and whose harvesting has been strictly, even severely controlled, have suffered less. Yet the days when you could take them with a gaff or a forked stick in shallow water have long gone.

Of the islands, only Grand Manan has been able to maintain a viable fishery but it, too, is suffering from the recent collapse of groundfish stocks. Herring, however, have remained remarkably faithful to particular weirs and lobster and scallops are still available. At Dark Harbour, on the west coast of the island, there is also a particularly pure form of dulse, a potassium-rich edible seaweed that is gathered off the rocks, sun dried, and sold to food stores and passing tourists. Grand Manan fishermen, too, have adopted aggressive and imaginative marketing policies for both fish and shellfish; they sell lobsters to German restaurant chains and mackerel and herring that are too large for canning to Russian factory ships.

SALMON FARMING ↷

BECAUSE OF THE GROWING SCARCITY of wild fish, attention is now focused on aquaculture, or fish farming, widely regarded as the only reliable means of harvesting fish in inshore waters. In the European world, the practice of impounding fish in coastal tanks and basins goes back to Roman times and beyond, but not until halfway through this century, when the Vik brothers in Norway began raising rainbow trout in marine enclosures, did Europeans attempt to farm fish with the same seriousness and on the same scale as we farm animals. The *andromadous salmonids* (salmon, rainbow trout, brook trout, and Arctic char), which can be raised in fresh water and transferred to salt, were natural candidates for the first modern experiments. And with their firm flesh and delicate flavour they could, like any good cash crop, command high prices in the marketplace.

The old and the new. In the background, smoke houses and storage sheds at Seal Cove, Grand Manan; in the foreground a circular salmon cage.

By the 1970s the princely, and more highly priced, salmon had ousted the trout from most sea farms, and the floating sea cage had taken over from the sea enclosure. In the wild, salmon spawn on stream beds and the young spend their first two or three years in freshwater before, as six-inch-long silvery smolt, venturing down to the sea. Breeding habits that were well known and relatively uncomplicated could be duplicated, if not easily. For years salmon have been raised in hatcheries to enhance wild populations, but culture stopped when the smolt were released in the sea.

From the fjords of Norway, the practice of taking hatchery smolt and rearing them in sea cages spread quickly to Scotland and Ireland and from there, in the late 1970s, to eastern Canada. Fears that Canadian waters, which get no help from the warm North Atlantic Drift, would be too cold for salmon were dispelled by successful government-supported experiments conducted off Deer

Island in 1978-1979. The great stirrings of the Bay may keep temperatures uncomfortably close to the lethal levels for salmon, but by mixing warmer waters with cold they also prevent the wide ranges of temperature that are lethal to finfish.

Commercial production quickly followed the Deer Island experiments and the industry, despite a chronic shortage of smolts through the early and mid-1980s, has never looked back. With no commercial hatchery in operation until 1986, smolts at first had to be supplied by the Department of Fisheries and Oceans, the Huntsman and the Atlantic Salmon Federation, and there were never enough to go around. But since 1988 commercial producers have been able to meet the demand.

The Atlantic salmon, despite its imperious ways in the wild and its susceptibility to stress when captive, has adapted to life in the sea cages. Gourmand fears that its flesh, no longer honed by epic wanderings in open seas, would become flaccid and tasteless, have also been confounded. Salmon swim in an endless circle around their pens and the treadmill leaves them almost as lean and well-muscled as their free-ranging cousins.

Unharried by predators and fed a regular diet of fresh fish or manufactured pellets, they also grow more quickly than wild salmon and they can be harvested (before they mature sexually) when their flesh is at its finest and firmest. By controlling temperatures and oxygen levels in the freshwater rearing tanks, growth in the early or smolt stage can be compressed into one or two years, and the cultured smolts grown to market size (3 to 5 kg) in sea cages in fourteen to twenty-four months. Under controlled conditions, grilse (a salmon mature enough to return from the sea to the river) can be produced from an egg in three years. In nature it takes at least four. In the case of salmon, culture is faster than nature.

On any listing of New Brunswick's assets, farmed salmon rank high. Within a circle of cold water circumscribed by Eastport, Deer Island, Back Bay (on the New Brunswick mainland) and Grand Manan there are now more than sixty farms. They range in size from small family operations with 25,000 fish to corporate undertakings with 250,000, and together they contribute more than

David Martin, netmaker, of Seal Cove, Grand Manan, making nets for salmon cages. Salmon farming has revitalized an ancient craft.

$100 million annually to the local economy from sales alone. Add the indirect benefits from associated industries producing smolts (young salmon sturdy enough to leave freshwater hatcheries for sea cages), fish feed, cages and nets, and the value of fish farming doubles or triples. The salmon harvest alone is now worth almost one-and-one-half times as much as the New Brunswick potato crop, and it virtually matches the landed value of lobsters, scallops and everything else caught by traditional fishermen along the New Brunswick coasts of the Bay of Fundy and the Gulf of St Lawrence. In Maine, too, where farmed salmon are second only to lobster in sea-food sales, aquaculture is rapidly overhauling the traditional fishery. Currently, there are thirty farms in the state, most of them in Washington County—Charlotte County's neighbour—generating an income of some $45 million.

Last, and by no means least in a region where an all-seasons job usually means working for government, salmon farming offers steady, year-round employment for about a thousand people. Salmon grow and feed in the warm season and are harvested between September and March. Cages have to be cleared of ice and seaweed, predators—chiefly harbour seals—kept at bay, and the fish monitored at all seasons.

FARMERS AMD FISHERMEN ↻

BUT AS WITH ANY NEW ENTERPRISE that edges into territory long claimed by old ones there are grievances and conflicts of interest. In the European countries, Norway in particular, fish farmers have been able to keep their distance from fishermen, but in the Bay of Fundy farmers and fishermen occupy a relatively narrow coastal zone. Contact, and conflict, was inevitable. The sheltered coves, bays and inlets where early fish-farming technology required aquaculturists to place their cages were precisely the locations where traditional fishermen harvest lobster, scallops and, if any are available, groundfish. Batches of stationary cages in a cove or bay restrict the area available for fishing and inhibit movement on the water.

As the cages move into more open waters where fast-running tides can flush away waste food and faeces, they compete directly with herring weirs; the optimum location for a weir is usually at the end of a point where the tide runs strongly. Weirmen complain that the cages not only block "fishways," and divert herring away from the coast, but that the noise, lighting, and uneaten herring-based fishmeal around the cages frighten them. The salmon is a herring predator and the herring is a nervous fish. The possibility of cages moving into even deeper water offshore, as inshore sites become increasingly scarce, has now alarmed groundfish trawlers and herring seiners who fear that in order to fish they may have to negotiate an obstacle course of salmon cages.

Territorial disputes aside, the most contentious issue raised by salmon

In fish farming, as in any other intensive form of animal husbandry, the two basic operations are feeding and cleaning. Here farmers at Greens Point, near the Deer Island ferry, clean nets.

farming is the threat posed by the wastes issuing from the cages. In summer, the growing season, young salmon feed voraciously. In locations where the tide runs strongly uneaten food and faeces get swept away but on "depositional" shores, where tidal currents are weak or flushing is inhibited, wastes accumulate. Cages must be moved periodically to allow the bottom to clear, or be cleaned, and oxygen pumped into the water to keep the stock healthy. Oxygen depletion can also be harmful to local plant and animal populations and unflushed waste, critics note, leaves an oil slick on the shore. Lobstermen and scallop draggers are afraid that wastes from the cages could damage spawning grounds, and clam diggers fear that they may wash onto intertidal flats occupied by the water-filtering, soft-shelled clam. Fish farmers, who seem genuinely puzzled by these concerns, argue that the first victims of damaging pollution will be their own fish. Growing salmon need large amounts of oxygen.

For waterfront property owners, the chief objections to fish-farming are aesthetic. Eyes that see only beauty in weirs and the weathered lobster-trap and gillnet buoys of the traditional fishery are offended by banks of geometric salmon cages (square, hexagonal or circular) and the strong colours and contours of the buoys and high-tech equipment associated with them. Plastic and metal, unlike old wood, can never acquire a patina. Some property owners, too, are upset by the regular arrangement of the marker buoys and the quality of the bird life around the cages; uneaten food attracts the scavenging seagull, not the lordly osprey or eagle.

Not to be outdone in the picturesque department by the traditional fishery, aquaculturists in Scotland and Norway—but not yet in Charlotte County—have begun to apply themselves to the aesthetics of fish farming. They can do nothing about the seagulls, but on their cages and equipment earthtones (browns, greys and blacks) are beginning to replace oranges, reds and yellows. Cages and marker buoys will be more difficult to see, but at least romantic eyes will not be offended. The final stage in the process could be picturesque, Reptonian arrangements of buoys and cages. Humphry Repton, a popular but demanding 18th-century designer of English country estates, insisted on having odd numbers of trees and shrubs, and even of cattle and sheep, in fields and pastures visible from the main house. Seven cows would "compose" whereas six would not.

Bruised sensibilities may never heal, but the abrasions produced by chafing between new enterprises and old, are for the most part surface injuries that time and effective management should eliminate. In small fishing villages there is a great tendency, as Joseph Gough, a thoughtful contemporary writer on the fisheries, has pointed out, to see anything new as the enemy. "Everywhere and always fishermen [have] tended to associate depletion with rival types of gear." As the latest type of gear, salmon cages are an inevitable target. To reduce levels of frustration in inshore waters, what seems to be needed is a system of zoning that will protect both the fisherman and the aquaculturist. In territorial disputes the needs of the aquaculturist, who is the protagonist, tend to get overlooked. But traditional methods of fishing or harvesting—eg. scallop dragging—conducted too close to the cages can alarm the salmon and, at times when the water is particularly cold (superchilled), cause mortalities.

Periodic disputes over territory and the dispersion of wastes are not to be taken lightly, but they ought perhaps to be regarded as manifestations of a deeper, seldom-articulated tension. As ways of life, fishing and fish-farming are polar opposites. The fisherman seeks to harvest a common resource, the fish-farmer to exercise proprietary rights over particular parcels of fish. All they have in common is the medium in which the fish live and grow. Fish-farming, as aquaculturists insist, is a type of agriculture, not an extension of the traditional fishery.

Fish-farmers are not given exclusive rights to patches of water but the effect of a bank of stationary cages with its attendant walkways and storage sheds is to exclude all other users. De facto property rights have been introduced to a domain that, in theory at least, has always been free. In practice, most coves and inlets have been the undeclared and unmarked preserves of particular groups or families, but a bank of steel cages is an unmistakeable badge of property.

Fish-farmers argue that in the Bay of Fundy the herring weir, which is a passive fishery, sets a precedent for the salmon cage. Staked to the bottom, weirs are absolutely immoveable whereas salmon cages are merely anchored. Weirmen, too, it so happens, are first in the long line of applicants for aquaculture licences. Defenders of the traditional fishery, however, retort that weir fishing, unlike salmon farming, is almost always a communal enterprise. Ownership of the weirs is shared so that a man who is part-owner of a weir might also set lobster traps, drag for scallops, seine for herring, or even dig for clams. Weirmen are never as specialised as aquaculturists.

Traditionalists also point to fundamental differences between the shape and structure of weirs and cages. More often than not the salmon cage is a stiff rectangle, made of plastic or metal, whereas the weir is a sinuous curve of

Earth-toned floats and cages have yet to reach Charlotte County, but old fishing huts loaded onto barges may soothe romantic sensibilities.

saplings that extends the line of the shore and simulates the natural arc of a fishway. It is more organism than mechanism. Festooned with seaweed, an old brush weir looks like an amphibious extension of the land. In the cultural and ecological stakes, the salmon cage is a non-starter.

To highlight the differences between aquaculturists and fishermen, the farmer/rancher dichotomy is often adduced. Aquaculture sites, the argument runs, are analogous to homesteads on open prairie. To keep stock in and predators out the sites are fenced and, like prairie farms, they are given up to monoculture. In effect, salmon cages are less farms than feedlots, but the point is

A barge on Deer Island loading supplies for a salmon farm at Indian Island, about half a mile away.

moot. Like many prairie homesteaders, most fish-farmers had no previous experience of farming and no expert knowledge of their environment. A few aquaculturists were once fishermen but beneath the oilskins of the fish-farmer you are more likely to find a former teacher, housebuilder, engineer, policeman, or even a professional footballer. Government support and research has been as necessary to aquaculture as it was to prairie farming, the various research and teaching establishments in St Andrews serving the same function as government experimental farms in the west. Not the least of these back-up services is an aquaculture technician training programme initiated by the Huntsman but now operated by the New Brunswick Community College at St Andrews.

The fisherman, on the other hand, is a natural rover—the phrase is Joseph Conrad's—thoroughly in tune with his environment. Just as a rancher on featureless prairie might pinpoint his location from the lie of the grass, the feel of the wind and the behaviour of his horse, so may a fisherman by the sound of the water, the patterns or "streaks" in its surface, the handling of the boat, and the direction of the rain. Like the rancher, too, the fisherman is capable of operating, if he has to, with a minimum of gear. His open boat, oars and handlines are the equivalent of the rancher's horse, stock saddle and lariat. Out in the Bay of Fundy herring are now taken with purse seines but older fishermen can still remember when they were rounded up or "driven" by open rowboats and dories.

Because the entire sea is his resource, the fisherman automatically resents any obstacle, physical or institutional, that inhibits his free and full use of it. Historically, his safety and independence lay in knowing the sea and being able to fish at will, taking groundfish or herring in one season, or one year, lobster and scallops in another. The ability to survive in a difficult and often dangerous environment is cause for pride: "A fisherman is what I would classify as the most independent man that ever lived. Because when you are out on the water, there's lots of times when you've got a decision to make and you can't talk it over with your neighbour. Whatever you do, your life may depend on it. And you've got to make that decision, whether right or wrong. And when you get ashore, you do the same thing." (Beacher Allen, Deer Island, 1983).

The struggle is invigorating. Beacher Allen again: "It gets into your blood, this fishing. I was over in Maine for a few years, and every spring I could smell copper painting and I wasn't within forty miles of it. And I'd get wondering whether the boys had the weirs built, whether the fish would strike before they got her ready."

That thrill of anticipation, peculiar to the hunter, may also become part of the folk memory of Passamaquoddy. Blessed by government and—romantic views of the wild fishery to the contrary—by the public at large, aquaculture is extending its range both geographically, by moving into areas previously considered too cold for salmon, and organically by embracing new species. Halibut, haddock, flounder, striped bass and lumpfish are all candidates for the sea cages.

In Passamaquoddy, experiments with haddock and halibut are well advanced. The first batch of hatchery raised haddock have survived their first six months in sea cages at Campobello, and as a farmed fish they seem set to rival salmon. Haddock, whose eggs are suspended in the water column, are more difficult to hatch than salmon, but because they are reared exclusively in salt water they grow faster. And, like the halibut, they may well have a higher tolerance for very cold water. Halibut, too, have now been raised in the hatchery from the egg to the juvenile stage and are ready to brave the sea cages. In Campobello, captured young halibut have done well in captivity; they seem less susceptible to disease than salmon and in the pens they grow as thick as footballs. There have been

Flat-bottomed motorized steel barges for serving the salmon cages are a recent addition to the coastal landscape.

similar experiments with cod in Newfoundland where fishermen are being trained to cage and fatten fish too small to sell.

Shellfish, too, seem certain to become an important part of the Passamaquoddy fish farmer's repertoire. Scallop culture is already underway in St Andrews and there is no apparent reason why mussel culture, which is well established in other parts of the Maritimes, could not be introduced to the Quoddy region. Mussels and scallops can either be suspended vertically in the water or they can be sown, as juveniles, on the bottom for later harvest. In Passamaquoddy, growth rates for shellfish, as for finfish, are excellent.

REFLECTIONS ON A LANDSCAPE

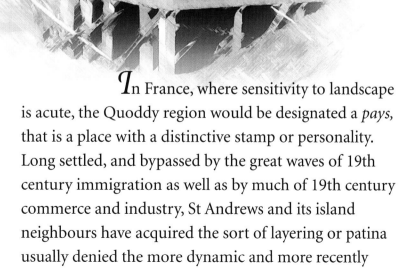

*I*n France, where sensitivity to landscape is acute, the Quoddy region would be designated a *pays,* that is a place with a distinctive stamp or personality. Long settled, and bypassed by the great waves of 19th century immigration as well as by much of 19th century commerce and industry, St Andrews and its island neighbours have acquired the sort of layering or patina usually denied the more dynamic and more recently settled parts of the continent. All landscapes can be interpreted, or read, but in one long settled and relatively undisturbed, the reading, or the peeling back of the layers, can be particularly satisfying. Walk through any town or village in the Quoddy region, or along almost any settled shore, and you will find aged houses and buildings, the remains of old fields and orchards, the stumps of old wharves, or the ruins of old boat sheds and canneries. It may not be Constable's beloved landscape of "mill-dams, old rotten planks, slimy posts, and brickwork," but in North America it is as close as we get.

Wander into a cemetery or open the local telephone directory and you find more evidence of long and, again by North American standards, undisturbed settlement. Inquiring eyes see not a potpourri of names from continental Europe, Asia and the Americas, but phalanxes, in stone or print, of Lords, Cummings, Calders, Guptills, Ingalls and Ingersolls. Eastern and Central European immigrants may have landed in Saint John but the C.P.R., with empty lands to settle and freight rates to collect, quickly funneled them into the golden West. Not, in any case, that a region that is little more than sea-girt rock would have enticed farmers from the Russian steppes or the plains of the Danube and the Vistula.

Ears, too, quickly pick up the distinctive notes of the Quoddy region. The broad, flat "ahs" of Eastport and Grand Manan are immediately identifiable, but everywhere there are echoes of the Old World in intonation and usage. What is said, too, may be as notable as the way of saying it. Much of the small talk is of the sea. Which weirs are taking herring, which clam flats are open or closed, the price of lobster and salmon, the iniquity of DFO regulations and quotas. In spring and early summer the talk shifts to "the season," of tourism, and all dependent upon it wait anxiously for the "flow" of tourists to begin. The annual insurgence brings in much needed outside money and, no less valuable in places where insularity is a built-in hazard, new ways, new blood and new ideas. Spring everywhere is a season of hope but in coastal places it has a particular zest. Buildings lashed by sea winds and salt air are patched and painted, often with strong, bright colours to counter the bleaching effects of wind and reflected

The Quoddy region's answer to Constable's landscape of "mill-dams, old rotten planks, slimy posts, and brickwork": an old boat sinking into the woods of Navy Island off St Andrews.

sunlight. On shops and hotels, summer awnings go up and baskets and window boxes gay with flowers are put out. Working boats, too, get a face-lift and pleasure boats, often stored in yards for the winter, are uncovered and trundled down to the shore. Out in the Bay weirmen hang nets and replace damaged poles, wondering as they do so if this will be the season when the herring strike and produce a truly silver harvest.

Spring also sees the return of retired or elderly natives who may have been south for the winter months. Returnees are very much part of this landscape, and not just those from the south. Every town and village has its quota of men and women who spent their working lives in Boston, Quebec, Ontario or the West and have come home again. They were pulled by the ties of family, of childhood friendships, and of a setting never out of the mind's eye. Missed were the sea, the heady smell of dank or rotting seaweed, and the pleasures, rarely articulated, of living in a landscape that developed largely in response to human needs, not to centralised or bureaucratic notions of how a landscape should be ordered.

On the islands and the peninsula, as in Maine and the Maritimes in general, roads go around hills and harbours instead of across them, streets have names, and towns and villages are where we think towns and villages ought to be: in valleys, at the ends of promontories or peninsulas, or at the heads of harbours and bays. It is a Rockwellian landscape of simple and obvious purposes. The older houses, too, look as if they had been built purposefully; most have porches for getting into and out of winter gear, steeply pitched roofs that shed the snow, large functional kitchens, and ground plans that may once have conformed to a pattern but have become eccentric. One of the pleasures of being home, as a friend and returnee from the West remarked, is visiting houses where you don't always know where the bathroom is.

As a place where buildings, and sometimes artifacts, are recycled rather than replaced, the Quoddy region's past is both continuing and evident. Residents and regular visitors hardly need reminding of this, but what until recently was merely understood has now received official sanction. In 1993 Charlotte County, of which the Quoddy region is the heart, was designated a Heritage Region, one of five in Canada. The idea of a heritage region came, significantly, from France where the aim was to turn the national interest in regional character to commercial advantage. Unable to compete with global competitors in the production and provision of standard goods and services, country places everywhere have to capitalize on the resources, skills and knowledge peculiar to the region; in short, on the natural endowment and the cultural inheritance. It is a lesson that the people of Charlotte and Washington counties, who have ridden the waves of political and economic misfortune, ought to learn very quickly. To promote products and services distinctive of the region, each Heritage region chooses its own identifying symbol or logo. It is a way of using heritage to heighten the sense of place and—the hoped for corollary—to unleash invention and enterprise. And the logo for Charlotte County?—an island-bound bay with a sailing ship, a seagull and a herring weir.

BIBLIOGRAPHY

Acheson, T.W. "Denominationalism in a Loyalist Country: a Social History of Charlotte County, N.B." Master's thesis, University of New Brunswick, 1964.

Bartko, Martha Ford. *Passamaquoddy, Genealogies of the West Isles.* Lingley Printing, 1975.

Brown, Donald C. "Eastport: a Maritime History" in *American Neptune* 28 (1968). Reprinted by the Border Historical Society, 1968.

Davis, Harold. *International Community on the St Croix.* University of Maine, 1950.

French, Hugh. "Sardines from Europe to Passamaquoddy, a Study in the Diffusion of Technology 1875-1899." Master's thesis, University of New Brunswick.

Grand Manan Historian. (An occasional publication of the Grand Manan Historical Society.)

Jack, David Russell. "St Andrews by-the-Sea" in *Acadiensis* 3 (1903).

Kilby, William Henry. *Eastport and Passamaquoddy: A Collection of Historical and Biographical Sketches,* 1888. Reprinted by the Border Historical Society, 1982.

Lorimer, J.G. *History of the Islands and Islets of the Bay of Fundy.* St Croix Courier, 1876.

Mowat, Grace Helen. *Diverting History of a Loyalist Town.* Brunswick Press, 1953.

Murchie, Guy. *St Croix: The Sentinel River.* Duell, Sloan and Pearse, 1947.

Nason, Roger. "Meritorious but Distressed Individuals: The Penobscot Loyalist Association and the Settlement of the Township of St Andrews." Master's thesis, University of New Brunswick,1982.

Nowlan, Alden. *Campobello.* Clarke Irwin, 1975.

Scherman, Katharine. *Two Islands: Grand Manan and Sanibel.* Little, Brown, 1971.

Walker, Willa. *No Hayfever and a Railway.* Goose Lane, 1989.

Wilbur, Richard. *Silver Harvest.* Goose Lane, 1986.

Wilbur, Richard and Janice Harvey. *Voices of the Bay.* Conservation Council of New Brunswick, 1992.

Wood, Pamela. *Eastport for Pride.* SALT, Inc., 1983.

Zimmerman, David. *Coastal Fort: A History of Fort Sullivan.* Border Historical Society, 1984.